The Romans

This book deals with five aspects of the archaeology of the Roman Empire. The first chapter describes how scholars and the adventurers began to study and explore the remains of Roman cities and towns in the lands around the Mediterranean and beyond. In the second, the author gives an account of present-day excavation at the Greek city of Knidos in the Roman province of Asia—in many ways typical of cities in the eastern part of the empire.

The author goes on to explain the work of specialists in different fields—coins, pottery, and inscriptions—and shows how each has different methods and how all of them make a contribution to our knowledge. This is followed by an account of the advances that archaeology has made in one particular and important subject: the Roman army. The author draws on material from Spain, Britain, the fortress city of Dura on the Euphrates, and especially the great legionary base of Lambaesis in North Africa.

Finally, a brief survey is given of a few of the outstanding surviving remains of Roman cities and engineering works in Europe, North Africa, and the Near East.

In a book dealing with such a huge subject the author has chosen to concentrate on certain topics in detail, rather than cover the whole field superficially, and to give the reader a first-hand glimpse of archaeologists past and present, their work and their discoveries.

Also in this series

EGYPT   Anne Millard
ROMAN LONDON   Ilid E. Anthony
THE GREEKS   John Ellis Jones

THE YOUNG ARCHAEOLOGIST BOOKS
Edited by Robin Place, MA, FSA

The Romans

MARK HASSALL

WITH A FOREWORD BY
SIR MORTIMER WHEELER

Drawings by Sian Bailey

Rupert Hart-Davis   London

Granada Publishing Limited
First published in Great Britain 1971
by Rupert Hart-Davis Educational Publications
3 Upper James Street, London, W1R 4BP

Copyright © 1971 by Mark Hassall

ISBN 298 79124 2

$A/ 913. 3 7'03$

Photographic Sources

Page 25, Mrs. J. Bradford (plate 38, J. Bradford, *Ancient Landscapes*,
Crown Copyright reserved); 18, 85, 88, British Museum; 90, 97, Ray
Delvert; 56, V. M. Conlon; 104, German Archaeological Institute,
Madrid; 34, 41, 44, Sheila Gibson; 99, 100, Photographic Giraudon; 28,
39, 62, Mark Hassall; 27, photo by J. K. St. Joseph, Cambridge University
Collections, Copyright reserved; 48, 55, (British Museum) Matthew Wade;
23, A. Poidebard (*La Trace de Rome dans le Désert de Syrie*, plate VI);
21, the original is in the British Museum.
 The author and publishers also wish to acknowledge that the illustration
on page 94 is adapted from the reconstruction by A. G. Drachmann, that
on page 57 is taken from fig. 25 of M. H. Callender, *Roman Amphorae*,
with the permission of the author and Durham University, and that on
page 82 is adapted from the plan by the late V. E. Nash-Williams in the
Bulletin of the Board of Celtic Studies, part II, May 1955, fig. 17, with the
permission of the University of Wales Press.

Contents

List of Illustrations

Foreword

Mr. Hassall's book is, within the meaning of the word, a book of adventure. It tells about the Romans, who once ruled a large part of the civilized world, and about getting to know the Romans by active exploration. Both subject and method are instinct with adventure, with intelligent discovery, which is not a bad definition of the word.

In appropriately summary fashion, the author begins with an outline of the emergence of methodical archaeology—as of other branches of science—in the eighteenth and nineteenth centuries, culminating in the development of "archaeology from the air" after the first World War. He then gives something like a three-dimensional actuality to his theme by taking his readers round the scene of an extensive excavation in progress. He chooses for the purpose a remote but famous site where he has himself worked with an international team for three years: the Graeco-Roman city of Knidos on the rock-bound coast of south-western Turkey. Here in the last century was found the lovely Greek statue of Demeter long familiar to visitors to the British Museum. Today under the spade the ancient city, difficult of access whether by land or by sea, is gradually assuming an intelligible shape, with its typical double harbour, its temples and theatres, its porticoes, houses and tombs. But our guide is, for the moment, more concerned with the Turkish workmen and their (mostly) European or American supervisors; with the human reactions and interchanges which are a basic factor in fieldwork of this kind and in no small measure determine its ultimate success. It is well that in an introductory essay of this kind the personal aspect should be stressed at the outset.

The author turns then to the specialist activities of numismatists, pottery experts and epigraphists, and finally gathers some of his threads together in a note on the Roman army and on features of Roman civic life. As a setting for the army he takes the great legionary fortress of Lambaesis in Numidia, and thence travels at leisure to Timgad, Pompeii and Provence, ending before the Maison Carrée at Nîmes. The book is an instructed tour rather than a treatise, and for that very reason the better fulfils its primary purpose. I gladly commend it to the young archaeologist.

MORTIMER WHEELER

Introduction

Men have always been interested in the past. Before the invention of writing, bards told tales of the deeds of men of old—often the ancestors of the kings and princes whose courts they visited and from whom they received rich rewards. The Romans too had their tales about the legendary beginnings of their nation, of Romulus and Remus, the brothers who founded Rome, and before them Aeneas, who brought the ancestors of the Romans to Italy as refugees from Troy. Even when Rome became a great world state, the Romans themselves remained intensely interested in the past. But such legends are not history; nor are they archaeology.

As soon as writing is discovered, the new invention at once finds a hundred uses. The deeds of great men are cut as inscriptions upon their tombs; business records are kept; treaties and laws are published on tablets of bronze for all to see. All these documents provide the raw material for the historian, who can supplement them, if he tells the story of his own day, by eye-witness accounts of the events that he describes.

The Greeks virtually invented the science of history—the art of piecing together and sifting through a mass of documentary evidence in an attempt to find out the truth. The Romans in turn learned to write history from the Greeks, although even the best Roman historians never equalled the best Greek writers of history. Yet neither Greeks nor Romans produced *archaeologists* in our sense of the word. The Greek word from which the English "archaeologist" comes means simply a person who writes ancient history. But in English usage an archaeologist is someone who reconstructs the past, not from historical documents, but from the physical remains of past civilizations, from material things like weapons and buildings, graves and potsherds. It never occurred to those Greeks and Romans who were interested in the past and all aspects of it that actual *history*—of a sort—could be written from stones and bones; that by studying such things, even past civilizations that had left behind no written records at all could still be made to speak; and that a vast amount could be learned even about past civilizations that had left records.

This book sets out to tell how long after the Roman Empire had crumbled in the dust, the science of archaeology began, how archaeologists started to study the remains of Rome's empire, first in Italy and then gradually exploring all the lands that border the Mediterranean—and beyond—for the ruins of Roman temples and cities, forts and roads. It goes on to describe something of the work of archaeologists today, what they can tell us about Rome's empire, and finally what still survives of the cities and buildings of one of the greatest super-powers that the world has yet known.

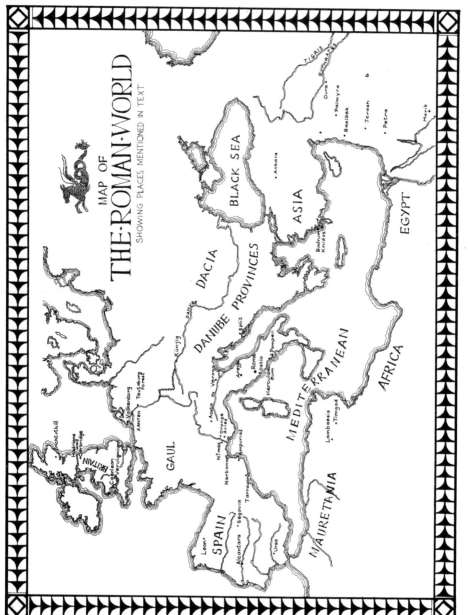

MAP OF
THE·ROMAN·WORLD
SHOWING PLACES MENTIONED IN TEXT

Map of the Roman Empire (only sites mentioned in the text are shown).

CHAPTER ONE

Explorers and Discoverers

Of all past civilizations, it was the classical culture of Greece and Rome that claimed men's attention first after the long night of the Middle Ages was over. This was no accident, for it was *The* in Italy that the new intellectual and cultural revolution first *Renaissance* broke out. In the fifteenth and sixteenth centuries A.D. Italy was the scene of intense artistic and scientific activity. It produced some of the greatest explorers, artists, architects, and astronomers that the world has known. Such men did not look back to the recent past before launching into the unknown, for the recent past could tell them little. Rather, they tried to rediscover what the Greeks and Romans had known about geography, the laws of proportion and the physical sciences, and then use this knowledge as a base from which to discover more. This period is known as the Renaissance because it saw the "rebirth" of all that was best in the old classical civilization.

At the same time, men of wealth and learning made collections of classical sculpture and inscriptions. They were the first of a long line of wealthy collectors that ranged from the Popes* to young English aristocrats who were sent on the "grand tour" of Italy as part of their education. Such men were not true archaeologists. They usually had more in common with the Roman generals and aristocrats who carried back Greek statues from Sicily and Greece (especially from the city of Corinth, which was captured and destroyed by Rome in 146 B.C.), or with the present-day millionaire collectors of French Impressionist paintings. However, the more serious-minded of these young noblemen did form themselves into societies like the Society of Dilettanti (founded 1733–34) and the Society of Antiquaries (which received a royal charter from George II in 1751, though it had existed before that date), which were later

* The great Vatican Museum was started by Clement XIV, Pope from 1769 to 1774.

to do excellent work. The first scholarly publications on antiquities too began to appear in the seventeenth and eighteenth centuries—such as Jan Gruter's *Collection of Roman Inscriptions*, printed in Heidelberg in 1603, or Jean Vaillant's work on *Roman Imperial Coinage*, which was sold out as soon as the first edition was published in Paris in 1682.

The first archaeologists

To most people, however, archaeology is something more than just publishing collections of Roman inscriptions or writing learned works on coins. It means digging, and the chance discoveries of Herculaneum in 1738 and Pompeii ten years later, followed by their partial excavation, more than any other event can be thought of as the beginning of what can be described as "dirt archaeology"—actual excavation. These two Roman cities near the modern city of Naples were of little importance in their own day, but the eruption of the volcano Vesuvius A.D. 79, which overwhelmed them both in lava and ash and so both destroyed and preserved them, has given them a fame far greater than many much larger cities. The excavation of these two sites showed dramatically that by digging in the ground it was possible to learn more of the everyday life of the ordinary Roman man in the ordinary Roman street than could ever be learned from the surviving works of Roman authors alone. Pompeii and Herculaneum were the first true excavations not only on Roman sites but on archaeological sites of any period. It is not surprising that those who carried them out for the young Queen of Naples were more like treasure hunters than professional archaeologists. It was not until a hundred years later, in the middle of the nineteenth century, that an Englishman working in Dorset developed the techniques of scientific excavation as we understand them today (this was the great General Augustus Pitt-Rivers). This book is not concerned with excavation technique as such, but this is a subject that will be touched upon in the next chapter.

Exploration and "fieldwork"

To most people archaeology means digging, but archaeology is not just a question of digging things up. There is also the question of discovering new sites in the first place. Almost every newcomer to an excavation asks those who are doing the work: "How do you know where to start excavating"? A frequent answer is that a site was discovered by chance. This is what happened in the case of both Pompeii and Herculaneum. However, many new sites are discovered not by chance at all but

14

as the result of a deliberate search. How then does one go to look for a Roman site, and how did enthusiasts do it in the eighteenth century?

In the eighteenth century much of the land bordering the Mediterranean—especially the North African coast, modern Turkey, and the eastern Mediterranean lands—was very little known and was also very wild. To find new sites in these areas did not require a particularly well-trained archaeological eye, but it did require great powers of physical endurance and courage. The modern archaeologist even in these same areas is much better off in some ways—the hardships and dangers have largely gone. But then most of the big and spectacular sites have been discovered, so, to make up, he has to be a much more skilful observer, or fieldworker as he is called by fellow archaeologists. The eighteenth and nineteenth centuries saw plenty of exploration but very little of the less dramatic but more skilful fieldwork.

The first—and really the only—true field archaeologist of the eighteenth century was a General William Roy. His field-work was carried out solely on Roman sites, and he used techniques of the highest standard, so that he certainly deserves mention in any history of archaeology—especially a book like this, concerned with the Romans. Roy worked in Scotland, where he had undertaken survey work for the government, and the story of his finds was eventually published in 1793, some years after he died, by the Society of Antiquaries, under the title *Military Antiquities of the Romans in North Britain*.

Like all educated men of his day, Roy was steeped in the classics, and it was therefore natural that for his study of the Roman army and its camps and forts in Rome's most northerly frontier province he should start with what the classical writers had to say. But it is in the third part of the book that Roy's skill as a fieldworker shows through and it is this part that is still of interest today. It is entitled the "Description of North Britain and the Camps Related to Agricola." Agricola was one of the most famous generals ever sent out to govern the province of Britain. He arrived in Britain A.D. 78, the year before the eruption of Vesuvius, and stayed until the year 84. His achievements were recorded by his son-in-law, the famous Roman historian Tacitus, in his *Life of Agricola*. Tacitus was chiefly concerned in praising the great man's virtues, not in

An eighteenth-century general on the track of Roman armies

15

Title-page of General Roy's classic book on Roman forts and camps in Scotland.

The half-title of Roy's book— a landmark in the history of fieldwork.

THE

MILITARY ANTIQUITIES

OF THE

ROMANS IN NORTH BRITAIN,

AND PARTICULARLY THEIR

ANCIENT SYSTEM OF CASTRAMETATION,

ILLUSTRATED FROM

VESTIGES OF THE CAMPS OF AGRICOLA EXISTING THERE:

HENCE HIS MARCH FROM SOUTH INTO NORTH BRITAIN IS IN SOME DEGREE TRACED.

COMPREHENDING ALSO

A TREATISE,

WHEREIN THE ANCIENT GEOGRAPHY OF THAT PART OF THE ISLAND IS RECTIFIED,
CHIEFLY FROM THE LIGHTS FURNISHED BY RICHARD OF CIRENCESTER.

TOGETHER WITH

A DESCRIPTION OF THE WALL OF ANTONINUS PIUS,
COMMONLY CALLED GRIME'S DYKE.

TO WHICH IS ADDED,

AN APPENDIX, CONTAINING DETACHED PIECES.

THE WHOLE BEING ACCOMPANIED WITH MAPS OF
THE COUNTRY, AND PLANS OF THE
CAMPS AND STATIONS, &c.

THE

MILITARY ANTIQUITIES

OF THE

ROMANS IN BRITAIN.

BY

THE LATE WILLIAM ROY, F.R.S. F.S.A.

MAJOR-GENERAL OF HIS MAJESTY'S FORCES, DEPUTY QUARTER-MASTER GENERAL,
AND COLONEL OF THE THIRTIETH REGIMENT OF FOOT.

PUBLISHED

BY THE ORDER, AND AT THE EXPENCE OF,

THE SOCIETY OF ANTIQUARIES OF LONDON.

———

LONDON:
PRINTED BY W. BULMER AND CO.
AND SOLD AT THE APARTMENTS OF THE SOCIETY, IN SOMERSET-PLACE; AND BY MESSRS. WHITE, ROBSON,
NICOL, LEIGH AND SOTHEBY, BROWN, AND EGERTON.

MDCCXCIII.

247230

16

writing a detailed account of the campaigns by which he finally crushed the resistance of the fierce highland tribes of Scotland. Roy realized that archaeology could help make good the gaps in Tacitus' account. He was a military man and had a soldier's eye for country. He could appreciate the military potential of a site. He realized, too, that however much the landscape may appear to have changed on the surface, the underlying structure of the countryside—the bones of the countryside, as it were—remains the same. His conclusion was that "it will appear evident that what with regard to situation was an advantageous post when the Romans were carrying on their military operations in Britain, must in all essential respects continue to be a good one now."

Roy, in recognizing this basic fact, used it to locate the sites of previously unknown Roman forts and camps. He wrote of the discovery of one such site, the romantically named Grassy Walls strategically placed on the banks of the Tay: "even the partial existence of this work gave great pleasure and was considered as exceedingly fortunate . . . from its being found where it was absolutely sought for." One can willingly allow the old general his pleasure!

It is this eye for country that makes the true field archaeologist. It is a rare gift, and good field archaeologists are probably much thinner on the ground than good excavators. Roy had no rivals until the present century. Interestingly enough, Roy predicted that traces of the Roman army would one day come to light in "the least cultivated districts of Africa, Spain and Gaul that were so often traversed by powerful Roman armies." He ruled out places where there had been intensive cultivation since Roman times, little guessing that one day air photography would make possible the discovery of new sites even in these areas. As far as Africa, Spain, and Gaul were concerned, camps and forts *have* since been found in all three countries, but when Roy wrote his discoveries stood alone. He realized that the reason for this was simply that no one had bothered to look. . . .

While Roy was trudging over the heather through the Scottish mists in the steps of Agricola's legions, far away from the centre of the empire, north even of Hadrian's great frontier wall, others were beginning to explore the Mediterranean lands. What discoveries awaited them! It is hardly surprising that the

The lost cities of the Empire

17

slight traces of the camps of the Roman army should escape notice when whole cities were waiting to be discovered. By the middle of the eighteenth century expeditions of travellers had already explored the coasts of Turkey. The Society of Dilettanti organized one expedition which visited, among other sites, Knidos, to be described in the next chapter. Their discoveries were published in a magnificent volume illustrated by superb engravings. Gradually it became possible to travel in the Middle East and North Africa, and the search for Rome's lost cities began.

One of the greatest and certainly one of the earliest of these explorers was Johann Ludwig Burckhardt, who died in 1817 in his mid-thirties, worn out by a life of hardship and adventure. Burckhardt was a Swiss, but he found financial support for his travels in Africa and the Near East from a British organization called the African Association. Since the Arabs were highly suspicious of infidel Christians, he learned to speak Arabic fluently, studied the Koran, wore Arab dress, and adopted the name Sheikh Ibrahim. In his travels Burckhardt visited the great caravan cities of what are now Syria and Jordan, including Palmyra. He was the first European ever to visit Petra—the legendary city carved out of the living rock, described by the poet J. W. Burgon, in one of the best-known lines of verse in the English language, as "a rose-red city half as old as time." Petra was originally the capital of a people called the Nabataeans and later became the capital of the Roman province of Arabia. It is still one of the most exciting places to visit in the whole Roman Empire.

Somewhat earlier than Burckhardt was James Bruce, a Scotsman who visited many of the sites in North Africa and Syria between 1763 and 1768. He was a giant of a man, six feet four inches tall, and had bright red hair. He was also very brave and had many adventures, including being shipwrecked off the Libyan coast. Unfortunately he also had a streak of vanity and boastfulness in him that made many people disbelieve his stories when he got home—especially his account of how he had gone in search of the sources of the Nile. His work as an observer of antiquities was good, even if he gives little credit to the Italian draughtsman who accompanied him in Libya.

Half a century after Burckhardt it was still necessary to   19

(*Opposite*) A nineteenth-century lithograph of Petra, the fabulous "Rose-red City."

A/ 913.3 703

penetrate the remoter parts of Arabia in disguise. In 1869 the Frenchman Joseph Halévy disguised himself as a Jew from the Yemen and visited the ancient city of Marib in the south of the Arabian Peninsula. The Yemen lies far beyond the borders of the Roman Empire, and Halévy's brave expedition would be out of place in this book if he had not had Roman predecessors. The land of the Sabaeans, in which Marib lay, had been a legend for centuries, for it was none other than the Biblical land of Sheba, whose queen visited King Solomon. To the Romans it was a far-off land that produced spices and gold. They called it Arabia Felix, Arabia the Happy and Blessed, and it was to them what El Dorado was to the Spanish adventurers in Central America. During the reign of the Emperor Augustus (27 B.C.–A.D. 14) a great army advanced across the deserts guided by friendly Nabataeans from Petra. Its commander was an officer by the name of Aelius Gallus, and his hopes must have been high as he marched with his men across the burning sands. However, sickness and the terrible heat proved too much for his men, and after fighting one or two skirmishes with the Sabaeans, few of them returned with him to the province of Egypt.

*"Gunboat"
archaeology*
The eighteenth and nineteenth centuries, then, saw the heroic age of the exploration of Rome's vast empire, before the invention of modern methods of transport, when every weary mile had to be covered on foot or camel-back. In the course of the nineteenth century the work became more and more scientific. For the British it was a period of "gunboat" archaeology. British naval survey teams did good work on the Turkish and North African coasts, noting the presence of antiquities besides their primary task of taking depth soundings and constructing charts, and when the Englishman Charles Newton (see the next chapter) set out for Knidos in 1857, it was on board the British naval vessel *Supply*. He borrowed navy personnel—a sergeant, six marines, and two engineers—as well as equipment such as lifting tackle and eight prefabricated wooden huts of the type used during the Crimean War. Newton's team also included a photographer, remarkable at such an early date.

The last of the great heroic endeavours undertaken without the help of jeeps and shortwave radio, at least, the last within the
boundaries of the Roman Empire, were the three American

A group of Newton's excavators at Bodrum (ancient Halicarnassus)
taken by his team's photographer.

archaeological expeditions to Syria carried out between 1899
and 1909 under the leadership of Howard Crosby Butler. Their
primary objectives were surveys of archaeological sites, map
making, and the recording of inscriptions—mainly written in
the local Semitic languages and Greek, for Greek was never
superseded by Latin in the eastern half of the empire and
appears even on many official inscriptions set up by the Roman
government. Like Newton, Butler's team published a straightforward account of the route they took and their everyday
experiences which makes exciting reading.

Shortly after the American expedition the First World War
broke out, and the world was not the same place again. In the
nineteenth century the European powers had established empires
for themselves in Africa, and by the time war broke out Spain, 21

France, and Italy had brought the whole of the North African coast under their control from the Atlantic to the borders of Egypt. The Arab lands round the eastern Mediterranean, however, remained in the hands of the Turks. After Turkey's defeat in the war, Egypt became an independent kingdom, and Palestine and Transjordan became British protectorates, while France assumed responsibility for Syria. The area was now wide open to study by European scholars and archaeologists.

There was a second new factor. As late as 1909, the American expedition had toiled in the wasteland of the Hauran, the stony desert south of Palmyra, using methods of transportation that had not been improved upon since the time of Burckhardt a hundred years earlier. The war, besides causing political changes, also brought about a technological revolution. Especially, it gave a great boost to aircraft development. Before the invention of the airplane it had taken months to explore the desert areas of the Middle East, and the exploration, however careful, could never be really thorough. None of those early explorers could ever be certain *what* lay behind each range of rocky hills that he passed by beside his line of march. Now it was possible to explore the same ground in a matter of hours as thoroughly as if whole armies of men had been used for the job.

It was not just a question of covering the ground quickly and easily. The quality of the survey work carried out from the air was much higher. It is strange to think that, despite the difficulties and dangers that they faced and the excellent work of recording that they did, even the American Syrian expedition was nothing more than a glorified sight-seeing tour as far as the techniques of fieldwork were concerned. In this respect they had not caught up with the standards set a hundred and fifty years before by General Roy.

The man to make the most of the new opportunities for aerial survey was a French priest, Father A. Poidebard. Poidebard flew numerous sorties over the desert, covering huge tracts of country swiftly and thoroughly. He could see details from the air that would have been either completely invisible from the ground or, even if visible, would have made no sense at all. Imagine the heaped rampart and defensive ditches of a Roman camp or fort. Through the ages the rampart has tumbled and the ditches have become silted up. Poidebard found that the

22

Father Poidebard takes to the air—400 metres above the Syrian desert.

silted-up ditches, because they had been cut through hard rocky ground, managed to trap some moisture in the dry climate. Where there was moisture patches of vegetation had a chance to survive, but where the ground was hard and rocky and where all that remained of the ramparts was scattered rubble, the lack of water meant that plants had no chance of growing. The pattern made by these patches of vegetation might be meaningless at ground level, but from an aircraft it would at once become clear, and so another fort site would be discovered. Again, Poidebard found that the low angle of the sun in the early morning or in the late afternoon caused even the most insignificant humps and mounds to cast long shadows. This meant that the destroyed and ruined ramparts and ditches of abandoned Roman forts could often be discovered by the long shadows that they cast, although they would have completely 23 escaped the notice of someone walking about on the site. Where vegetation of any type might be altogether ruled out by the lack of water, this shadow method of discovering new sites was especially important.

While Poidebard was perfecting the techniques of aerial photography on the eastern frontiers of the empire, the pioneer in Britain of this new form of archaeological research was O. G. S. Crawford, the archaeological officer attached to the Ordnance Survey. To explain what the Ordnance Survey is and how it got its name, one must go back to the reign of Henry VIII, when a part-military, part-civilian organization called the Board of Ordnance was formed. The job of the board was to supply the needs of the army with everything from cannons to the Tudor equivalent of paper clips. By the end of the eighteenth century there were still no really reliable maps of the British Isles, and so the Board of Ordnance, which was responsible for these too, undertook its own survey. Since then the survey has had a permanent staff working for it, constantly bringing its maps up to date and adding all conceivable sorts of information to the maps. Crawford was the survey's first "archaeological officer." He at once saw the value of air photography in locating new sites. The principles of air photography in a country with a wet climate like Britain and many other parts of Europe are rather different from those which apply in countries with an arid climate like Syria. In Syria it was the presence or absence of vegetation that was significant. In a place like Britain it was differences in the way the vegetation grew that mattered. The extra moisture and richer earth in buried ditches cause crops to grow more luxuriantly and to remain greener during the hot summer months, while where the ground is stony, the crops will not grow so well and, if the summer is hot, they will tend to become parched. Air photographs clearly show up these differences. An air photograph of a fort like that on page 27 shows the ditches as dark lines and the internal streets between the different barrack blocks as white lines.

More political upheavals   The Second World War resulted in political changes similar to those that had been caused by the First World War. The old European colonial powers were weakened or defeated, and a new spirit of nationalism swept through the Arab countries. In North Africa British General Bernard Montgomery had defeated German General Erwin Rommel and his Italian allies,

24

Centuriation in the Po valley of northern Italy; modern tracks and field boundaries preserve the rigid grid pattern.

and Libya, which had been under Italian control, passed for a time into the hands of the British. In the Middle East a new state, Israel, was created out of Palestine, and the old protectorates gradually asserted their independence.

During the war air photography of military targets had played an important rôle in areas where there had previously been no archaeological air photography. In Libya, British archaeologists did good field surveys, largely using wartime air photographs. They also studied wartime photographs taken over Italy, Yugoslavia, and Tunisia, and saw with astonishment something that had never been apparent from a casual glance at ordinary maps, something which shows as clearly as anything could the logical and orderly Roman mind. In all these countries Roman land surveyors had been at work long before. They had divided the agricultural land of the cities by a series of roadways intersecting each other at right angles so as to form huge grid patterns. The squares between the roadways were known as centuries—Latin *centuria*—because they contained a hundred subdivisions of two Roman acres each, originally thought of as the allotment of one peasant. This system of land division is known as centuriation. Chance has preserved a collection of Roman technical works on land surveying, so that the way the Roman surveyors went about their work is clearly known. The principal instrument that they used was the groma, a staff with a wooden cross mounted like the arms of a signpost. The arms of the instrument were kept horizontal by watching the small weights attached to the ends of the arms by threads. When they hung parallel to the upright staff, the staff itself was vertical and the arms of the crosspiece were level. By sighting along the arms the land surveyors could mark out right angles on the ground. The actual remains of a groma have been found at Pompeii.

This groma— surveying instrument—belonged to a surveyor called Verus who lived at Pompeii nineteen hundred years ago.

Meanwhile, the French, who had been pioneers in the aerial survey of military remains on Rome's eastern frontiers, were not idle. The work of Poidebard in Syria was followed by similar work in North Africa by a fellow countryman, Colonel Jean Baradez. Baradez explored the Roman frontier works in Algeria. There a continuous ditch (*fossatum*) marked the boundary between the nomad raiders of the desert and the empire, where farmers could live and work in comparative peace on the fringes of the desert. Besides the ditch, there was a whole com-

26

Glenlochar, site of a permanent Roman fort in southwest Scotland. The streets between the buildings show up as white lines— the ditches as dark lines.

plementary system of military roads, police posts, and fortified farms, the Roman predecessors of the present-day semi-military farming settlements on the borders of Israel.

In Britain, Crawford's work has been followed by that of Dr. J. K. St. Joseph. In the south of Britain, St. Joseph discovered fort sites in areas of intensive cultivation, where General Roy believed traces would never be found. He also flew over the Scottish lowlands and up the eastern flank of the highlands, where Roy had laboured so many years before. His discoveries often confirmed suggestions made by the old general and added enormously to the total number of known sites of forts and the temporary camps built each night by Roman armies on campaign. Sometimes a number of these camps appeared to be so similar in layout and overall size and were so regularly spaced apart—between half a dozen and a dozen miles—that they were obviously part of a single series. St. Joseph realized that now, for the first time, *it was possible actually to follow the course of a Roman army on the march and point out on a modern map where their actual camp sites had been each night.*

The importance of air photography cannot be stressed too   27

much. As we have seen in the wilder parts of the Roman *Ground surveys*
Empire, aerial survey is the only practical way of covering
enormous stretches of country, and both in these desert areas
and in the agriculturally developed countries of Europe, features
that would otherwise never be visible at all show up to an
observer in an aircraft. However, it would be wrong to think
that fieldwork today just consists in taking photographs from
an aircraft—*surface* investigation plays a very important part,
too. It takes the form of noticing the slightest trace of ruined
walls or the scatter of potsherds and broken tile where ancient
settlements once existed. This is something that anybody can do
in any country, but to be most effective it can be organized on a
team basis. Here the British schools and institutes of archaeology
in Athens, Baghdad, Ankara, and Rome have played a particularly important part in organizing and co-ordinating research.
The British school at Rome was opened in 1901. It caters for
different interests, but it is also naturally more concerned with
Roman archaeology than the others and acts as the base for
British archaeologists working in Italy.

In looking for new sites the fieldworker neglects no clue that *Place-names*
may help him. Sometimes these can be found in old maps that *and other clues*
mark forgotten boundaries or lanes that follow the arrow-
straight lines of Roman roads. Sometimes they can be found in
place-names. The Roman word for "camp" is *castrum* (plural
castra). The barbarians, Germans, Celts, and Arabs, on the
borders of the empire, heard the name and tried to pronounce it
their way, and so the English word *chester*, the Welsh word
caer, and the Arabic word *gasr* came about. The presence of
any of these words as part of a place-name may well show
that there was a Roman fort on the spot. A field near the
ancient Biblical site of Megiddo in present-day Israel bears the
name Lejjun—the only indication that this was indeed the base
camp of a *legion*—VI Ferrata, the "Ironsides." It is the exact
equivalent of the name of the Spanish city León—the base of
Legion VII—and of Caerleon (Welsh = the camp of the legion),
the base of Legion II Augusta stationed in South Wales.

Sometimes the barbarian settlers who invaded the empire
forgot who the true builders were of the ruined temples and
tombs that they found. These seemed to them strange and
mysterious places, certainly the homes of unpleasant creatures
and probably of evil spirits. This way of thinking is reflected in   29

(*Opposite*) Gasr Wat-Wat—a Roman-type tomb at Germa, capital of the
legendary Garamantes, who lived in the Libyan desert beyond the
imperial frontier

the new names they gave the old Roman works. For example, the local name for the Roman frontier wall in the province of Rhaetia (southern Germany) is the *Teufelsmauer*—the devil's wall—and the Arab name for the Roman-type tomb illustrated on page 28 is *Gasr Wat-Wat*, the Castle of the Bats.

So it is that place-names, just as much as potsherds, grassy banks, or shadows seen from a low-flying aircraft, can tell the experienced fieldworker that the Romans were there before him. This chapter has covered a great deal of ground. We have ranged from one end of the empire to the other in space and from the Renaissance to the present day in time. We have learned how the archaeologist knows where to dig. The next chapter shows something of what is involved in the actual process of digging—what it is like to dig on a Roman site.

CHAPTER TWO

Life on an Excavation

There is probably no such thing as a typical excavation, and this is as true of excavations on Roman sites as it is on sites of any other period. However, the *sort* of work that archaeologists do and the techniques they use are basically similar wherever they are at work. This chapter shows something of these techniques—and something, too, of life on one particular excavation—at the site of the city of Knidos in southwest Turkey. For three years, during the summer excavating seasons of 1968–70,. I was lucky enough to be involved in the excavations carried out by the archaeological department of the University of Long Island, and the description that follows is based on my own personal experiences. But, first of all, a general word about the site itself.

Knidos must in many ways have been typical of the cities of the eastern part of the Roman Empire, which at its greatest extent, in the second century A.D., stretched from the Straits of Gibraltar in the West to the Euphrates and beyond in the East. In the east there were cities much older than Rome herself and empires much older than Rome's had flourished. The last of these was the empire of Alexander the Great, who lived from 356 to 323 B.C. His conquests stretched from his native Macedonia as far as India. After Alexander's death his empire was divided into a number of kingdoms, each ruled over by one of his generals and their descendants. The form of Greek civilization that existed in these kingdoms is known as Hellenistic because it developed from the civilization of the golden age of Greece, or Hellas, whose highpoint was the fifth century B.C. The Knidos that was incorporated into Rome's new province of Asia (formed shortly after 133 B.C.) was a Hellenistic city similar to dozens of others in the eastern Mediterranean. The only respect in which it differed slightly from many of its neighbours was the particularly favourable

Knidos—a Hellenistic and Roman city

31

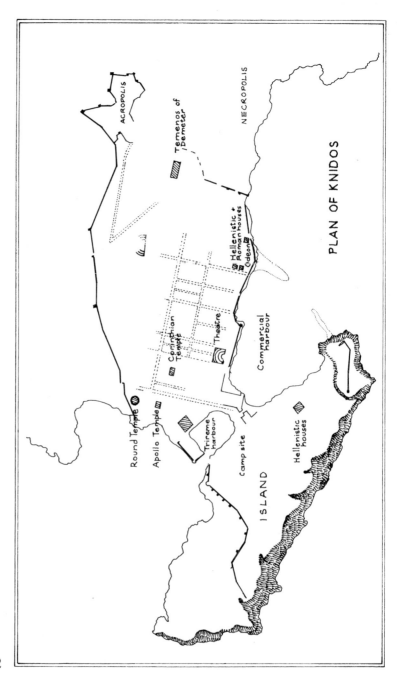

PLAN OF KNIDOS

ACROPOLIS

Temenos of Demeter

NECROPOLIS

Hellenistic + Roman houses
Odeon

Corinthian Temple

Theatre

Commercial Harbour

Round Temple

Apollo Temple

Trireme harbour

Camp site

ISLAND

Hellenistic houses

treatment it received from Rome. It had been an ally even before the formation of the province and afterwards was still treated with friendship as an old ally rather than as a conquered city. At the end of the republican period of Rome's history a citizen of Knidos, a certain Theopompus, had become a friend of the great dictator Julius Caesar (100–44 B.C.). As a result, during the early empire created by Caesar's nephew and heir, Augustus, the city received favourable treatment from the emperors. It is not surprising, therefore, that although many of the ruins which the visitor to Knidos sees date from Hellenistic times, some, including some of the most spectacular, are of the republican or early imperial period—that is to say, of the first century B.C. and the first two centuries A.D.

Knidos is situated at the extreme western end of a long *A city with* peninsula, at the extreme southwest corner of the landmass of *two harbours* Asia Minor (see map, page 12). It is very difficult to get to except by sea, for the land journey is over a long and winding road often built on the edge of high cliffs that fall nearly sheer to the blue of the sea below. But the country has a wild and evocative beauty that is hard to put into words, and this is highlighted by the very inaccessibility of the place. The city was built partly on the mainland, partly on what had once been an island. The two had been linked by the Knidians by a mole, and the construction of this resulted in the creation of twin harbours in the lee of the island. The two harbours were at one time connected by a channel so that ships could pass from one to the other. Normally, however, the smaller, westernmost harbour was reserved for ships of war; the eastern for the larger trading vessels loading cargoes of Knidian wine and other commodities. The eastern harbour opens onto the Mediterranean with its distant view of the isle of Nisyros; the western to the Aegean with shadowy Kos dominating the horizon. Our tents were pitched on the isthmus which linked mainland and "island."

My job in this delightful spot was to act as the assistant to the director of the dig, Iris Cornelia Love, of Long Island University, known affectionately in the Turkish press as the "mini-skirted professor." It involved touring the different parts of the ancient city of Knidos currently under excavation and helping the supervisors on individual sites with particular problems that might crop up. In describing a typical day on the 33

General view of the eastern harbour looking towards the island. At the far end of the bay is the camp site on the low isthmus.

excavation, I can do no better than to take the reader with me on my rounds for a conducted tour of the site. But before setting out there is the agony of getting up. . . .

How to wake up in south-west Turkey

Somewhere far off, and yet all too close, comes a raucous braying of trumpets—or so it seems to my sleepy senses, as they struggle upward into the realm of consciousness. And then I realize these are not trumpets but the dawn chorus of the donkeys of Knidos. These donkeys are regularly prohibited from the site and as regularly introduced by some of our workers, who ride them over from the neighbouring village of Yasiköy on Sunday night and back after the week's work on the following Saturday. Around me in the green half-light of the tent my companions are stirring: bearded and lanky David, one of our surveyors; serious and erudite Philip, king of the pot shed; and witty Rolf Stucki, a young Swiss archaeologist. As with campers the world over, our own corners of the tent have taken on something of our personalities. My corner, for example, is the epitome of squalor—an untidy heap of dirty clothes and swimming things, polythene bags of nuts and dried figs, shaving equipment, books, pieces of pumice stone, and suntan oil. Philip's is a haven of order. A small pyramid of reading matter, surmounted by a clock, rises from the foundation of his suitcase, in which, reposing like some Egyptian pharaoh of old, lie his clothes, neatly folded, clean and clinical. Philip is a fund of unlikely knowledge and has a mind like a computer. He can tell you where magnetic north was in 300 B.C. or how many Coca-Cola bottles placed end to end would stretch from here to the moon. I know because I asked him.

A whispered word comes through the fly sheet in the refined accent of Summit, New Jersey, from Marie Keith, librarian of the New York Frick Art Reference Library and administrative assistant on the excavation, which means she has a herculean task. She tells me that a new day has truly started.

Breakfast: boiled eggs, tea, bread, cheeses. We eat in front of the dig house, a rectangular stone building overlooking the eastern harbour. In one end of this building our two Turkish cooks—Mehmet, the lighthouse keeper, and Halil, the general factotum—perform miracles with the aid of Orşe Ullman, who is part Hungarian, part Greek, and a fluent Turkish speaker. The other end acts as a store for finds and equipment and there Philip has his office where he registers incoming finds. I eat a small breakfast in silence as usual, but across the table Hacki Bey, official representative of the Turkish Antiquities Department, is already laughing and joking. I watch the sun rise above the peak of the small mountain on the mainland where the citadel—the acropolis—of the ancient town once stood. As it rises, the shadows creep visibly down the rocky slope of the island opposite, and I know it is going to be another long hot day.

Each day begins with the same ritual. Iris Love, very dashing in sun helmet, slacks, and desert boots, calls out the names of the workers standing on the threshold of a half-completed building that will one day become a little restaurant. The workers answer as their names are called. Many have the same first names—we have several Alis, Mehmets, and Husseins.

Sometimes no one answers, and a friend explains that he is ill or we see a figure of a man who has overslept sprinting toward us from the rough shelters that the men have built out of branches. In the hot summer nights these are fine, although they tend to attract the unwanted attentions of scorpions. These nasty little creatures, however, turn up almost everywhere so that after a while one stops worrying about them.

Through Orşe, the interpreter, Iris tells the men to go back to the sites where they were working yesterday. While she makes her way back to camp, I hitch a lift with Marie Keith in the Land Rover out to the necropolis—the vast, sprawling cemetery that stretches along the road leading to the city.

The Necropolis —city of the dead

Marie is exploring a subterranean tomb chamber, unfortunately robbed of any rich offerings that it might have once held, but still very exciting and worthy of the meticulous records she keeps of her work. Nearby stands a beautiful marble drum-shaped altar decorated with carved ox skulls between which hang lifelike garlands of marble flowers. An inscription in Greek records the name of the man whose body once rested in the tomb. Marie's men work calmly and efficiently, and there are no problems here. One of her men has a sun-browned and wrinkled face, close curly hair, bright eyes, and a shrewd half-smile. In this setting of sunshine and olive trees, bare rocks and blue seas, he always reminds me of the wily, long-suffering Ulysses.

I lower myself gingerly into the tomb chamber and flash a torch at the recesses that once held the bodies of the tomb's owner and members of his family. The past seems very close. Above my head there is only a small patch of blue sky to remind me of the world of sunlight and air, and the voices of Marie and her workmen come to me from a great distance. They remind me that I must be on my way.

The walk back to the city is one of utter beauty. On my right rises the mountain spine of the rocky peninsula, grey, crumbly limestone, part cliff, part tumbled boulder and scree. On my left the land falls away steeply to the sea, sometimes dropping sheer to the blue water, sometimes to miniature beaches of shell-sharp sand. On both sides of the hot, dusty road are scattered olive trees and rough, cleared patches of corn. Yet the scene is not that of a well-ordered countryside, but rather of a garden run wild. Everywhere one can see the stumps of half-buried walls of fine, skilfully built polygonal or rectangular masonry, and behind the scrub one catches glimpses of black hollows—the mouths of broken tombs. For a few blissful minutes I am alone with my thoughts and the summer sounds of bees and cicadas. Some massive blocks stand out right by the roadside. I look up. Here the modern trackway breaks the line of the old city wall.

To the traveller entering Knidos from the east one of the first things he notices is, far up on his right hand, a sheer cliff of smooth grey rock, so smooth that it looks as if it must have been shaped artificially. But no, some titanic movement of the rock has split the mountainside as though with the single blow of a mighty axe. To the people of ancient Knidos there was something uncanny about this great cliff, and it was here that Chrysina, the daughter of some wealthy citizen, dreamed that the god Hermes told her to build a sanctuary to the goddess Demeter and her daughter, the underworld goddess Persephone. Here, two thousand years later, the British archaeologist Charles Newton came with his Turkish workmen and British marines from the frigate *Supply* and found the inscription that recorded Chrysina's gift and the statue of the goddess. Below, toward the sea, I can see the stepped seats of a small horse-shoe-shaped theatre—the south odeon. This little building was also investigated by Newton in the nineteenth century, but although last season we too did some work there, replanning the stage and auditorium, there is no work there now, and so, with a quick glance downward, I pass on into the town.

The sanctuary of Demeter

This area was once one of the residential quarters of the city. Like most Hellenistic cities the plan of Knidos was based on a rectangular grid of streets, only sometimes, where the ground sloped up steeply from the sea, the cross streets took the form of long flights of steps with landings at intervals. Above the flank of the hillside with its stepped streets, the ground levelled off to form a long narrow plateau, where the city architects encountered no such problems, before rising steeply again—in places almost vertically—to the rocky mountain of the acropolis. The roadway up to this citadel had to take a zigzag course, and even then its construction must have been a very difficult undertaking.

The first excavation site I come to is being supervised by Carol, an American girl who speaks Turkish fluently. It is lucky   37

Men at work   that she does and that she is intelligent and hardworking, for this is one of the most difficult areas under excavation. Carol has about a dozen workmen with her. I can see them now, hard at it beside one of the stepped streets. Her men are at work digging away the earth that covers the remains of houses. One of the difficulties here is the removal of the excavated soil. Some of this soil the workmen take away in wheelbarrows— good new wheelbarrows with pneumatic rubber tyres brought by truck all the way from Izmir, a long day's journey away by road; but the expense is well worth it, for nothing can be achieved without the right equipment. Others are shovelling earth downhill onto the roadway. As each shovelful lands, it throws up a cloud of dust that looks from a distance like a shell exploding. One solitary workman stands covered with dust on the roadway itself and shovels the earth farther on downhill to get it out of the way. He is bored with his task. I grin at him, say hello in Turkish, and hope that his work will go easily. He grins back and answers in English, "Good morning. How are you?"—obviously one of Paul Steinfeld's star pupils (you'll meet Paul later). "Fine, thanks. How are you?" I reply, adding in pidgin Turkish, "Much dust, very bad," and then for good measure, "You're Hercules." We both laugh, and I climb the steep stone staircase to say hello to Carol.

The work of a   Carol is industriously writing out labels for the wooden boxes
site supervisor   in which the workmen put the pottery they find. Each box has a label on which is written a letter code to show from which part of Knidos the finds come, a trench and layer number. The pottery is one of our most valuable guides to dating the buildings we uncover, and it is essential to know exactly where each piece comes from, whether it lay above or under a floor, or whether it was just a chance find. Beside Carol are a number of packets and polythene bags for "small finds." This term has a special meaning for an archaeologist and is used for anything which is not just ordinary, everyday pottery. In the bags today are a couple of moulded lamp fragments, a large-headed bronze stud, which was probably used to tack down ornamental leatherwork on a piece of furniture, and, more exciting, several small fragments of marble sculpture. Each small find has a label attached to it, similar to those in the pottery boxes, describing exactly where each was found.

38   Carol is excited because she has made an important dis-

Mud-brick partition wall of Hellenistic house at Knidos. In the centre of the wall is a blocked doorway (*see arrow*). To the right is a small niche for a statue.

covery on the lower part of the site, near the spot where I spoke to Mehmet, the solitary shoveller. Most of the houses in this part of Knidos were built in stone, but the Hellenistic building that fronted the modern roadway had internal walls of mud brick covered in painted wall plaster. When this particular building fell into ruin, the upper storey, which also had mud brick walls, collapsed into the semi-basement room below, and it is a tricky business for the excavators to discover what *exactly* is mud brick *in situ*—that is, in its original position— and what is simply collapsed mud brick debris. It is only when we are faced with the problems of mud brick walls that excavation at Knidos can pose problems. Carol had been carefully cleaning down the surface of one of these mud brick walls— which the workmen had already uncovered to its full surviving depth of some two metres—when suddenly she came to an area where there was no wall. She had discovered a doorway completely blocked with a jumbled mass of fallen mud brick which the workmen excavating on both sides of it had thought to be wall. The doorway was standing to its full height, though not surprisingly the courses of mud brick above had sagged downward when the wooden lintel that had once supported them had rotted and decayed.

Mud brick usually collapses into a heap of earth when a building is abandoned, so it is very exciting to find such a wall still standing to room height. The decoration, where it survives on these walls, is quite simple—large panels of yellow and white plaster—but then this was only a semi-basement room. The first-floor rooms above must have been much more impressive, and from their walls we have a great many fragments of painted plaster, some with elaborate interlaced patterns and meanders or miniature scenes with cupids and others showing fights between centaurs and Lapiths. The centaurs were legendary beings, half man, half horse, and the Lapiths, who were human, were their neighbours and rivals. There are also some elaborate architectural fragments in stucco.

Modern comforts in ancient Knidos

Farther up the hill was a second house, this time well built out of stone. It was supplied with water from an underground cistern water-proofed with plaster and had a large number of rooms, three of special interest. One of the rooms was square and entered by four doors, one in the middle of each wall. It seems to have served as a small reception room or hall. In one corner we found a collapsed marble table supported by a single pillar in the form of a herm, or bust, of Dionysus, the Greek god of wine. A second room was probably a reception room. A raised dais at one end had a simple mosaic floor, and the plastered walls of the room were ornamented with fluted stucco pilasters. The third room contained a bath—a deep, square, marble-lined tank in which the bather would have sat. The plumbing was impressive. The bath was filled by water under pressure which came up a lead pipe set vertically on the outside of the tank. A second pipe of terra-cotta would have taken the waste water away. The houses in this part of the city, both the masonry one just described and the house with walls of mud brick further down the hill, were not built on a particularly large scale, but they indicate an extremely civilized and comfortable way of life.

40

Farther along the modern roadway one comes to one of the most spectacular monuments to be seen at Knidos, the theatre. The theatre is architecturally something of a mixture. Like a true Greek theatre, but unlike most Roman ones, it has been partly hollowed out of a hillside. Here were set the horseshoe-shaped superimposed steps of marble that formed the seats of the cavea—the auditorium of a classical theatre. Where the two ends of the horseshoe project beyond the hillside, they are supported by massive retaining walls of squared masonry. There are other features about this building that bring it more into line with Roman theatres—the two vomitoria, or vaulted passageways, that lead onto the cavea from arched entrances cut through the retaining walls. At the foot of the cavea was a D-shaped open area, the orchestra, originally the place where the chorus performed sacred dances. On the other side of the orchestra was the raised stage, at Knidos built over three concrete vaulted passages. Again, a high stage built on a vaulted superstructure is typically Roman. Finally, behind this came the decorated façade of the stage building, which served as scenery.

The theatre

Part of the seats of the theatre. The dark opening at the left is one of the vomitoria. The stage and stage buildings are at the bottom on the right.

41

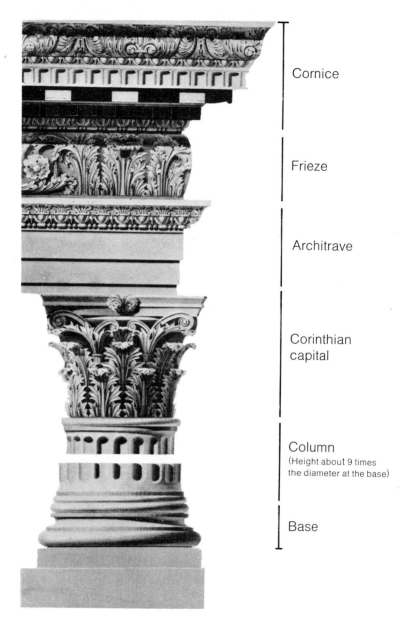

Cornice

Frieze

Architrave

Corinthian
capital

Column
(Height about 9 times
the diameter at the base)

Base

Engraved reconstruction by the Society of Dilettanti of some of the architectural detail of the Corinthian temple. Compare the Maison Carrée, page 101.

This was pierced by three doorways. Convention demanded that the centre door was used when the building was supposed to represent a palace.

Work in the theatre is fairly straightforward, for here it is only a question of clearing away the rubble and rubbish of centuries that has accumulated in the circular basin of the cavea and uncovering part of the foundations of the stage building. The only problem in fact is the massive size of some of the blocks of masonry and boulders that have fallen down into the orchestra on the collapse of part of the highest rows of seats. As a result, we use more workmen on this site. There are almost twenty of them under the command of a very capable Turkish girl, called Ilknur, who is a student of archaeology at Istanbul. Some of her men are busy clearing away earth and rubble with long-handled shovels and our good Izmir wheelbarrows. Others have fastened a block and tackle around a huge boulder in the bottom of a trench, making it fast to another, yet more massive, near the edge and then hauling it up a ramp made of two great baulks of timber. This can be very tricky work, but the Turks are very practical and delight in overcoming this sort of challenge. There is much shouting and heaving, and I lend a hand on the rope before going over to talk to Ilknur and an English student, Tony, who is with her. She is sitting on one of the lowest steps of the cavea near a large block, the base of a statue long since lost or broken. On it has been cut a Greek inscription that says:

> The people set this up to the gods
> In honour of Dionysokles, son of Drakontomenes,
> Because through word and deed he performed acts
> Of greatest service to the city.

The next sites to visit lie farther up the hillside and look down over the larger eastern harbour. To reach them, I climb the seats of the cavea and then follow a little winding goat track which leads up the hill. Here on a lofty terrace with a wide outlook to the south and west stood a beautiful temple. The capitals that crowned the columns were decorated with acanthus leaves finely carved in marble—the so-called Corinthian capitals, which became very popular during the Roman period. The concrete core of the high podium (the platform on which the temple was built), which was covered by thin slabs of marble veneer, the deeply undercut acanthus-leaf decoration 43

Preliminary work at the site of the Corinthian temple. More elaborate
equipment is needed before progress can be made.

of the capitals of the columns, and the scroll design of the
architrave all are indications of a Roman date. The temple has
been known for a long time and was visited by members of the
Society of Dilettanti at the beginning of the nineteenth century.
Work there during the previous year has modified their reconstruction in detail, but it is correct in general outline.

Without heavy lifting equipment it is not yet possible to move
the fallen columns and recover the plan of the internal arrange-
ments of the temple. Instead, work on the terrace is concentrated farther to the south. There a long and impressive
colonnade ran for a distance of about 120 metres, along the very
edge of the terrace. It consisted of a wide, spacious paved corridor down which people could stroll while protected from the
fierce heat of the sun. At the same time they could look out
over the harbour and "island" through the open south side, for
here the roof was supported on columns—some forty or so—
with fluted sides and flat plain tops in the Doric style. Un-

44

fortunately most of the portico has been robbed, its columns rolled downhill to be taken away by sea for building material or used in the construction of field walls. However, the building is of extreme interest, especially as it may be one mentioned by the Roman writer Pliny. He says that there was at Knidos a famous hanging portico—that is, one that was built on the edge of a cliff or terrace—that had been built by the famous architect Sostratus, a citizen of Knidos who lived at the same time as Alexander the Great. His most famous work was the Pharos, or lighthouse, at Alexandria, which was one of the wonders of the ancient world.

A young American girl, Margot, is in charge of work on the portico. By digging trenches to locate the foundations of the building at certain points, she is finding out its exact dimensions. Then our Irish architect, Sheila Gibson, will make a reconstruction drawing of the whole building, based on the plan that has been recovered and the fragments of columns that we have found. For this season work has almost come to an end, and I now show her how to draw the sections—diagrams of the sides of the trenches—so that we can see later exactly which layers are contemporary with the construction of the building (the make-up layers of rubble on which the marble floor once rested) and which layers are later (the rubble destruction layers above). Datable finds of pottery, etc., from the make-up layers are all-important, for they will tell us approximately when the portico was built and, therefore, whether we are justified in attributing it to Sostratus. The section drawings are as important as the plans when it comes to interpreting and studying the season's work later. We first fix a piece of string, the datum line, horizontally to two nails stuck in halfway up the side of the trench at each end. We use a spirit level that can be hung on the datum line with hooks to get the string perfectly level—when the line is horizontal, the bubble is central.

Drawing sections

A spirit-level.

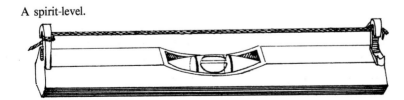

Parallel to the datum line a tape measure has been fixed, again against the section face, and Margot takes offset measurements with a steel tape at regular intervals along the tape to points where one layer ends and another begins. These points are then transferred to graph paper and connected so that an accurate diagram of the section face can be produced.

The friendly Turks   I make sure that Margot has no problems and then pass a word or two with the workmen. Many of them are old friends of mine and worked with me when I was a site supervisor in charge of a single site last year. They are a merry crowd, Mehmet Sönmez (küçük Mehmet, little Mehmet, we call him to distinguish him from the numerous other Mehmets), tall, gangling Fevzi Balle, Şükrü Korkut, with fine dark Arab features, Ilhami Akdeniz, with his red shorts. . . . We have one or two standard jokes at which we all laugh. Fevzi, who is a great one for merrymaking, takes me aside. He has a moustache and has not shaved for a week. He wears only a flat cap and long shorts. "*Bugün akşam biz beraber, restoran, çok şarap, çok bira*"—an invitation spoken in a husky voice in the pidgin Turkish, which is the only form of the language I can understand, to come drinking with him tonight. "*Belki, Fevzi, belki*" —"perhaps, perhaps"—I answer as I disengage the old rascal's hand from my arm and make my way over the broken columns of the once noble building to a lower intermediate terrace just below the one on which the portico once stood.

A Byzantine church   This lower terrace does not seem to have been built on in Hellenistic or Roman times, probably because building here would have detracted from the appearance of the portico behind it. In the sixth century A.D., during the Byzantine period, the site was thought too good to waste, and an imposing church was built on it, largely out of re-used pieces from the deserted Greek and Roman buildings. The task of clearing the church of the rubble from the collapse of the upper part of the walls would be an immense job, but earlier in the season we did undertake a limited amount of work here, and found that the aisles were floored in mosaic and the walls painted with figured scenes.

Within half an hour I have seen monuments from three great periods of Knidos' history—the Hellenistic portico, the Roman Corinthian temple, and now the Byzantine church—for Knidos, 46   like many a Roman city in the East, had roots in the past, and after a period of prosperity during the heyday of the Roman Empire, survived as a Byzantine city after Rome itself had fallen. During this time, like any city today, she had not stood still, but new buildings had arisen as old ones had been demolished or decayed, for cities, no less than the people living in them, are living organisms. Like people, too, they eventually die, and Knidos today is a dead city, though beautiful in her ruined desolation. Thoughts like these go through my mind as I pick my way over the fallen masonry to where Cathy is busy making a beautiful drawing of one of the mosaics. The mosaic is largely destroyed, but enough survives to show that it once was divided into squares by a plaited-braid pattern. In one of the panels were water birds, and one is cleaning its foot with its bill. It is important to draw the mosaics, as well as to photograph them, since there is much detail that is lost in a black-and-white photograph (such as would probably be used for publication) of a subject whose design depends largely on colour differences. The supervisors and workmen are backed up all along the line by people like Sheila Gibson, the architect, and Cathy, one of our draughtsmen, and others whom we shall meet later. Their work of recording is vital, and without it all the work of the excavators would be in vain. At the end of the excavation we shall put cement around the broken edge of the pavement to prevent more of the little square stone tesserae from coming out, while the pavement itself will be covered by sand to protect it from being broken up by the winter frosts. This can easily be cleared away if we come back to work in the Byzantine church again next season.

From the Byzantine church I follow a little track to another temple site, this time occupying a terrace at the extreme western end of the temple, overlooking the western harbour, as well as the open sea with distant Kos on the skyline. The temple here was dedicated to Apollo, as we know from an inscription. This is one of my favourite sites in the whole city. I acted as supervisor on this site in 1968, and as well as the beautiful view over to Kos, there are always cool breezes from the sea here, and on some of those burning summer days in Turkey they can be wonderfully refreshing. The temple itself, however, was destroyed in Byzantine times, and a small Byzantine church was constructed on the podium, or temple platform. Indeed, Byzantine Knidos must have been a city of

More temples

47

Later work at the "Round Temple" shows that it is indeed the Temple of Aphrodite or Venus—Iris Love's greatest discovery. Notice the earth baulks running out onto the temple platform. These will later be removed.

48

churches, for these two are not the only ones known. Later the material from this church was also robbed, and some of the great blocks forming the podium were heaved over by the local villagers to steal the lead from the clamps that the original builders had used to bind the blocks together. It is only now that we and our workmen can appreciate the fine workmanship of the original temple platform for its own sake. The supervisor here is Nermin—like Ilknur, another Turkish student. It is while I am with Nermin that one of our cooks, Halil, comes with a container of cold tea for us and everybody has a ten-minute break.

On the cliffs above us I can see small figures clearing yet another temple site of bushes before trenches can be laid out. I know that Iris Love will be there so that there will be no problems. Iris discovered the site only the day before, and what is particularly exciting is that enough showed above ground for her to be able to tell that the temple had a circular plan. Now this is interesting because circular Greek temples are rare anyway, but what is even more exciting is that the most famous temple of all at Knidos, that in which Praxiteles' famous statue of Venus stood, was probably circular since the statue could be seen from all sides. Could this be that temple?

After our ten-minute break I set out again. This time my path winds downhill, past great ruined cisterns and fig trees, past the one good spring at Knidos which provides water for the workers and the camp-site. Sadly it no longer bubbles out of the rock but has been covered by a concrete boxlike structure which looks completely out of place beneath the old mulberry tree that once sheltered the spring. My goal is the western harbour, the so-called Trireme harbour, where I find Paul, one of our best supervisors, and Martin, the site photographer, who are both Americans. Paul, like Carol, speaks fluent Turkish. He worked with the Peace Corps in Izmir before coming on the dig. "Hello, Professor," he says, grinning, as I make my way up to him. We decide on what shots Martin should take of what trenches. Each view will be taken in black and white and 35 mm colour slides. In each shot will be one or more metric ranging poles to act as a scale, and Martin will make a careful list of each site and trench he photographs and from which angle each photograph is taken, with other details such as aperture, shutter speed, type of film, etc. Once again it is the work of

The Trireme harbour

49

recording, whether by photography, drawing plans or sections, or labelling finds, that is vital.

There remains yet one more site. Rolf Stucki is working on the "island", and to get there I pass both the Museum—the stone building which serves as a drawing office—and the camp-site where finds are cleaned and marked. Lonnie, our young American surveyor, emerges from the Museum carrying the theodolite and its tripod, followed by young Mustafa with a surveyor's staff. The theodolite consists of a small telescope that can be held horizontal by adjusting screws on the top of the tripod on which it is mounted, until the bubbles in the spirit levels set into the machine are central. By sighting through the telescope and reading off the height on the staff held vertically by Mustafa, Lonnie can tell the relative height of any given spot to the place where the theodolite has been set. By taking many hundreds of such points Lonnie has been able to build up a contour map of Knidos, so that the individual sites that we excavate can be marked on an overall plan in their correct positions. Lonnie's work is of vital importance. Besides making a contour plan, he has marked on streets and buildings where-ever these can be seen without actual excavation. If there were no excavation done at Knidos at all, his master plan would still be of great value.

Inside the Museum I can hear Hazel, one of our draughtsmen, singing. She is at work drawing pottery. Her drawings will be added to the many hundreds that Cathy has already done, and these will be used to build up a type series of pottery forms (see Chapter 3). Outside are some of the larger finds, architectural fragments (decorated capitals and similar pieces of carved marble), marble sculpture, inscriptions, etc. I look wistfully at one of these. It has some thirty or forty lines of closely written Greek, some of them badly weathered, and I have spent all my free time trying to make an accurate transcription of it. However, I must hurry if I am to see Rolf's site before lunch.

On the way to Rolf I pass the camp-site. Here Philip and a band of helpers are at work registering and labelling small finds and pottery and giving special treatment to some of the more fragile objects (conservation). There are two Turks, an old man and a boy, busy washing pottery. Philip is Iris Love's second-in-command in the pot shed, just as I am in the field, and his work there could fill a whole chapter by itself. Some of its aspects are dealt with more fully in Chapter 3.

Rolf's site is in many ways similar to Carol's for he too is excavating Hellenistic private houses on terraces overlooking the larger, commercial harbour. His houses, however, are situated on the other side of the harbour on the so-called "island," and because they are almost entirely of stone rather than mud brick, there are not the problems of excavation that Carol had. Nor do they appear to have been so richly decorated—we found here none of the exciting painted wall plaster or marble sculpture. David, my other tent mate, is with Rolf and, helped by him, is making a detailed final plan of the site. I am still with them when the morning's work finishes. We shall now return to camp, have lunch, and swim, read, or sleep during the heat of the early afternoon before returning for another three hours' work. *A house with a view*

Such could be a typical morning's work at Knidos. Though no two excavations will ever be alike, the activities that I have described above will be the same on any excavation. First of all, there is the actual excavation, in this case done almost entirely by our excellent Turkish workmen. Second, there is the work of recording: the construction of an overall site plan, of individual site plans, and, of course, photography. All these are done by trained archaeologists and other specialists. Then there are detailed trench plans, drawings of sections, and the recording and registering of finds done by the supervisors. Last, but not least, there is the processing of the finds afterward in the pot shed, as it is always known, and the drawing of pottery, small finds, architectural reconstructions and plans. These are the elements that remain constant on any excavation, and without them the excavation itself would be barren labour.

CHAPTER THREE

Archaeological Specialists

There are many kinds of archaeologist at work studying Rome's great empire. There are the fieldworkers and aerial explorers whose activities we mentioned in Chapter 1. There are the excavators like those at Knidos whose job it is to uncover the remains of Roman buildings and discover actual objects. Then there is a whole range of specialists who are concerned with different aspects of the archaeology of the Roman Empire —people who study coins (numismatists), people who study inscriptions (epigraphists), and pottery experts. Finally there are specialists who study Roman wall painting and sculpture and Roman architecture.

This chapter shows something of the methods of some of these different archaeologists and something too of the way in which their work helps us to understand more about the Romans and their empire.

COIN EXPERTS

Coins are such a large and specialized subject that no attempt is made here to cover the whole field even briefly. In this section, instead, a short account will be given of the *sort* of information that the coin experts (numismatists) can give us about the life and history of the Roman Empire and of the part they play in helping the excavator "date" the building periods on his site.

Coin commemorating the capture of Jerusalem by the Romans.

The Romans used coinage in the way that modern governments use stamps—to commemorate important events and anniversaries. Take for example the famous coins issued to celebrate the Roman victory after a great revolt in Judaea in the first century A.D. On one face of the coin is the head of the Emperor Titus and on the other a palm tree; on one side of the tree is a Jewish captive with his shield and helmet and on the other a weeping woman. The Latin words *Judaea Capta* mean

Judaea Taken; and *SC* stands for *Senatus Consulto* (issued by decree of the Senate).

Other famous coins show the Colosseum, the great amphitheatre in Rome and the harbour at Ostia which was built by order of the Emperor Claudius. The figure at the top is a statue of Neptune that stood on the lighthouse built at the entrance of the harbour. The reclining figure below with a rudder and a dolphin represents Father Tiber.

This coin shows the Colosseum, the biggest ampitheatre in the Roman world.

Coin showing the harbour of Ostia.

Besides recording actual events and objects, coinage was used as a way of getting across simple ideas and messages to the people of the empire. It was used, in other words, as a means of spreading government propaganda. Here it had a great advantage in an age when there were no newspapers, radio, or television. Everyone handles money, and even those who couldn't read could always understand the simple message of the coins, which was also expressed pictorially.

The emperors naturally wished their subjects to be reasonably contented and happy—after all, a really bad emperor had an unpleasant habit of ending up with a dagger in his back—so they stressed the pleasanter side of imperial rule. *Pax* (Peace) often occurs, represented as a female figure with an olive branch and a sceptre. There may be *Annona*, the corn harvest, shown as a female figure holding corn ears and a horn of plenty, with a corn measure and the prow of a ship beside her. This symbolized the corn that was imported annually to Rome and distributed free to the citizens. Sometimes these simple messages must have fallen rather flat. If a coin type celebrated *Concordia* (Harmony) or *Fides Militum* (the Loyalty of the Soldiers), it meant often that there was civil war or that the soldiers were mutinous. The coins show what the emperors wanted people to believe was the case, and not necessarily the truth.

From these few examples it can be seen that coinage has a lot to tell us about events and conditions in the empire. But to the excavator, Roman coins are mainly useful when found securely in a layer—"stratified" is the technical term for this—they help him know the date of the layer. Even after Christianity was accepted as the official religion by the Emperor Constantine at the beginning of the fourth century, the years were not reckoned from the birth of Christ, so Roman coins do not have dates on them as modern coinage does. Instead, they

How to tell the date of a Roman coin

53

showed what year of a particular emperor's reign it was by the mysterious letters *TRIB.POT.* followed by a number. *TRIB. POT.* stands for *Tribunicia Potestas* (the power of a tribune). This meant that the emperor had the authority of one of the most important of the old Roman magistrates—the tribune. It was by holding this power among others that he was legally entitled to rule, and unlike his other powers, it had to be renewed each year. So *TRIB. POT. III* on a coin would mean that the emperor had received his *third* grant of the tribuneship and that it was the *third* year of his reign.

Even when a coin is very worn, it is often possible to tell from the emperor's portrait at least which reign it belongs to, for the portraits on the coins are very distinctive. By the fourth century A.D., however, they become very formal and are not so much help. But the subjects on the other side of the coins make it still possible to pin down the date of a coin.

How coins help to "date" a site   Coins then are very useful to the excavator who wishes to "date" his site. If a coin is found buried beneath a mosaic floor for example, the excavator knows that the floor must be *later* in date than the coin. But how much later? It all depends on how long the coin had been in circulation before it was dropped. This is really a matter for the expert, but there are two general rules. The first is that a worn coin will obviously have been in circulation for much longer than a coin in mint condition. Second, coins that are worth more than their face value— because the metal from which they are made is worth more than the official value of the coin—will quickly be snapped up by collectors and so pass very rapidly out of circulation. The reverse is true, and coins that people don't like get passed on and stay in circulation. This is the principle that "Bad money drives out good," known as Gresham's law. The most famous examples are the silver coins issued by Mark Antony before 30 B.C. The silver in these coins was so debased that they remained in circulation for more than 200 years, and consequently by themselves are a very unreliable guide for dating.

POTTERY EXPERTS

Roman pottery, like Roman coinage, is a complete subject in itself. It is possible to tell much about how pottery was made and how it was traded and so on, and all this is of 54   interest. At the same time, pottery, like coins, is extremely useful

Part of a mould for making Arretine pottery, and below a modern cast taken from it in plaster of Paris.

to the excavator anxious to date the buildings he uncovers.

Any excavation of a Roman site—especially a town site—will result in a great deal of pottery being found. Large-scale excavations at a city like Knidos, for example, will produce *tons* of the stuff. The reason is that clay when fired to make pottery is practically indestructible, though it is very brittle. So pottery breaks easily and often has to be replaced, but it is never completely destroyed as organic material, such as wood, bone, or leather usually is.

How can this mass of pottery be studied, and what can be learned from it? A casual glance at one of the finds boxes on the side of a trench at Knidos would show you that pottery sherds can be divided into two sorts. There are some sherds that come from finely made pots. The sides of these vessels 55 are often as thin as a modern teacup and can have a moulded decoration. The surface, too, may be painted or given a shiny black or red glaze. On the other hand, much of the pottery will consist of great thick sherds from larger vessels with no decoration at all. These will have been used for humble tasks in the kitchen. The archaeologist refers to the first sort as fine ware and the second as coarse ware. This broad difference between fine ware and coarse ware will hold good on practically any Roman site.

Now to produce fine-ware vessels or pottery lamps was a specialized job that took time and skill. As a result, small factories sprang up where there were craftsmen who had the necessary skills. Particularly famous in the late years of the republic and early years of the empire was the fine pottery made at Arezzo in north Italy. This pottery had beautifully moulded decoration and a glossy red surface. Later imitations of Arretine ware were made all over the empire, the so-called red-slip wares of the Mediterranean and the Samian pottery of western Europe—especially Gaul. A great deal of Samian, like Arretine, was elaborately decorated with designs of men, plants, and animals. In both cases these designs were produced by using a pottery mould—something like a cake or jelly mould, on the inside of which designs were stamped. Some designs were used exclusively by the same potters, and when even a tiny piece is found, it is sometimes possible to recognize it as the work of a particular man. The actual names of these craftsmen are known, too, because they included their names in the

Roman oil lamp. The wick which floated in oil came out of the large hole. Oil was poured into the smaller hole by means of a funnel. The scene on top shows a fight between gladiators.

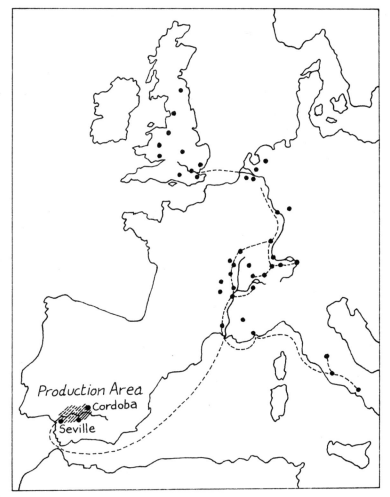

"Distribution Map" of find spots of amphorae stamped with the name of G. Antonius Quietus, showing the extent of the trade.

Production Area

Cordoba

Seville

decoration on the mould or stamped the pots with them before firing. The factories specializing in making clay lamps also frequently stamped their products.

It was not half so difficult or complicated to make coarse-ware vessels. These could be made wherever suitable clay was available. Because crates of pottery are very heavy and costly things to transport, kilns for making coarse-ware pots tended to spring up wherever there were towns or settlements to provide a market, and coarse ware as a general rule was not 57 exported from one place to another. An exception to this principle are the great storage vessels for wine, olive oil, and a sort of fish sauce called garum, known as amphorae. These amphorae were made on the estates that produced the commodities they contained and were then exported with them to wherever there was a market. The amphorae have the names of the owners of the estates stamped on the handles. Finds of these stamped handles at different sites allow archaeologists to plot the extent of the markets reached. We know, for example, that wine from Knidos was extremely popular in the eastern Mediterranean. It is possible to mark on maps the sites where amphorae produced on individual estates have been found, and so discover how far they were traded. However, the amphorae are exceptional among coarse ware, and by and large it is true that fine ware produced in the same factory will be found on a large number of sites, often quite far apart, while coarse ware will be exported only to sites in the immediate area of its manu-

Amphorae and distribution maps

A "type series" of amphorae. Changing fashions at different times and in different places result in distinct styles of these great storage vessels.

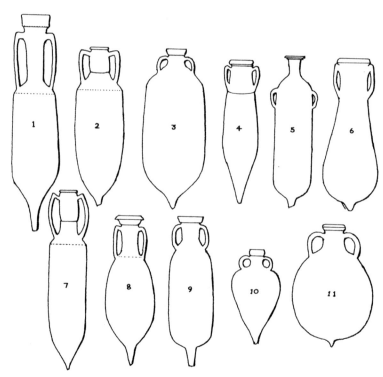

facture. The sort of coarse pottery produced by these numerous small factories tends to vary from region to region, so that the coarse pottery produced at one end of the empire will be different from that produced at the other.

A type series

Both coarse ware and fine ware have one thing in common, however. Over the years people became bored with the old shapes, and gradually the forms changed. There are fashions in pottery just as there are fashions in clothes. This means that the sort of pottery that the excavator finds at the lowest and earliest levels of his site will often be different from the pottery that turns up in the upper, later levels. Sometimes it is a question of gradual changes in the shape of a particular kind of vessel; sometimes a completely new shape will be introduced which will at first be found alongside the older shapes and will then gradually replace them.

The pottery expert working at a site like Knidos draws all the varieties of shapes of pot that are met with on the site. The illustrated "catalogue" of pottery shapes that he produces is called a type series in the technical language.

The pottery expert's next job is to give dates to the different pottery types. Rough dates are easy. He knows that pottery types that are common in the lowest levels on a site are earlier in date than the ones in the upper levels. Some of these levels he can date by coins. Luckily the fine wares can often be dated independently from evidence from other sites, and so the fine wares too can be used to give dates to the coarse-ware type series.

This is possible because the fine wares, the amphorae, and lamps were exported so widely. Now some of the sites on which these are found did not, like Knidos, remain occupied for centuries. They start or finish at a fixed point in time. The classic example of this is Pompeii, which ended literally with a bang in the summer of A.D. 79. Sometimes sites are known to have started at a particular date, so Augustus founded the city of Augusta Praetoria (Aosta) in 25 B.C. and there are many others. These sites are dated, not archaeologically, but independently by the writings of Roman historians, and are very important, for they provide the clues by which we can accurately date the fine wares and amphorae that are found there.

In a house at Pompeii, for example, was found an unopened crate of 90 Samian ware vessels made at factories in southern

Gaul. These pots must have reached Pompeii before the great eruption of Vesuvius in A.D. 79, but probably only a matter of days or weeks before, because the crate was still unopened. Similarly one of the amphorae exported by G. Antonius Quietus was found at Pompeii and must have got there before disaster overtook the city.

Pompeii, however, is an exceptional site. It is, in general, military sites such as forts that can be closely dated by historical record or inscriptions to a brief period of time. Particularly useful are the series of forts and camps built under the Emperor Augustus in the Lippe Valley in Germany in 11 B.C. and the years immediately following. These forts had a relatively short life. In A.D. 9 there was a great disaster in Germany when three legions were wiped out and many forts were stormed and burned to the ground. The forts that were not destroyed then were all abandoned five or six years later. The short life of these fort sites means that fine wares such as Arretine pottery found on them can be pretty closely dated.

"Dating" pottery   The pottery expert works from the known to the unknown. He knows the period when fine-ware types were common from historically dated sites. When he finds these fine-ware types whose date he now knows, together with coarse-ware types on sites which are not historically dated, it gives him the clue he is looking for to date the coarse wares.

The work of the pottery expert is now complete. He has worked out the full range of pottery types, for both the coarse wares and the fine wares, and he has produced a type series. He has gone through archaeological reports of other sites and worked out the dates for the different forms in his type series. The excavator can now use the type series as a work of reference and guide in dating the pottery he finds in any particular layer.

THE EPIGRAPHISTS

The word "inscription" comes from a Latin word which means something that has been written on something. The English word "epigraphy," which means the study of inscriptions, comes from a Greek word which means exactly the same thing. People who work on inscriptions are known technically as epigraphists.

60   For some strange reason the Romans set up inscriptions on

stone and engraved inscriptions on bronze on every occasion
imaginable. Like us, they set up milestones. They also set up
statues of famous men on bases that were inscribed with a summary of the man's whole career. They set up tombstones,
sometimes with lengthy inscriptions, and altars to their gods.
They inscribed the decrees of the emperor on tablets of bronze
and set up inscriptions on public buildings. They also wrote
things on walls just as much as people today—advertisements
and election slogans, not to mention vulgar comments. As one
wit scrawled on a wall at Pompeii covered with election notices:
"I wonder, O wall, that you have not fallen down in ruins from
supporting the silliness of so many scribblers!"

All these types of inscriptions are a rich source of information for the historian, and some of the most important of them
deserve to be ranked alongside the works of the great Roman
historians themselves.

The most important of all Latin inscriptions comes from
Turkey and has been called by the great nineteenth-century
German scholar Theodor Mommsen "the Queen of Latin
Inscriptions." This is the very lengthy inscription set up in both
Latin and Greek on the walls of the temple dedicated to the
Emperor Augustus at Ankara. Ankara, the modern capital of
Turkey, was known to the Romans as Ancyra, the capital of
the Roman province of Galatia, and for this reason the inscription is sometimes known as the Monumentum Ancyranum. The
inscription lists the achievements of the dead Augustus and was
written by the old emperor himself when drawing toward the
end of his life. Augustus was very anxious that future genera-
tions should get his version of the events of his reign and left
careful instructions that the account of his achievements should
be set up on two pillars of bronze in front of his tomb in Rome.
These have long since disappeared, but copies were also erected
in different parts of the empire, and the only copy to survive
almost completely is the Ankara inscription.

At the same time historians have to use the "Achievements
of the Divine Augustus" with care. Augustus was concerned to
present his reign in as favourable light as possible. Awkward or
discreditable events are passed over quickly or left out
altogether. An example is the disastrous expedition of Aelius
Gallus into Arabia (page 20). He says that large forces of the
enemy were killed in battle, many towns were captured, and the

army advanced into the territory of the Sabaeans as far as the town of Mariba. He *doesn't* mention the terrible losses that Gallus' army suffered on the return journey.

Fascinating as the information that can be gained from inscriptions is, it is the historians and not the archaeologists who really benefit, so that a long account of Roman inscriptions and what we learn from them would be out of place here. It will be enough to give three examples of typical inscriptions, each of which is of special interest.

The first comes from Caesarea Maritima, the seaport capital of the Roman province of Judaea. It was found in 1961 by Italian archaeologists and had been set up to commemorate the building of a Tiberieum—a shrine to the Emperor Tiberius. The name of the governor is given in the second line and the fact that he was *Praefectus Judaeae* in the third line. The *PRAEF* on the left of the stone at the beginning of the third line is missing, but the restoration is certain. The governor's name in the second line is also not complete. Only the letters . . . *TIVS PILATVS* survive. But it does not need the world's greatest epigraphist to restore the first name as *PONTIVS*. . . .

Inscription set up by Pontius Pilate.

The second inscription was found at Xanten, one of the legionary fortresses on the Rhine (page 66). It is the tombstone of a man called Marcus Caelius who came from Bologna in north Italy. He was a centurion in Legion XVIII and was killed at the age of fifty-three. The inscription set up by his brother says that he "fell in the Varus campaign" and expresses the hope that one day it will be possible to recover the dead man's bones. This is a reference to the terrible disaster of A.D. 9, when the governor of Germany, Quintilius Varus, perished with three whole legions in the sinister Teutoburg Forest. Marcus is shown carved on the tombstone with his military decorations on his chest and in his hand the vine staff that was the symbol of office of a centurion. On either side of him are the busts of two freedmen—slaves whom Marcus had freed and who perhaps accompanied him on that last fateful journey into the dark forests of Germany.

Finally another tomb inscription—from the eastern empire. It was carved above the doorway of a rock-cut tomb in Petra that once looked like the famous Treasury there (page 19). Over the centuries, howling desert winds have sand-blasted it so that it is now only a tortured ghost of a once-noble building. 63

(*Opposite*) Entrance to the temple of Rome and Augustus at Ankara. On the wall at the right was carved the famous "Achievements of Augustus."

The inscription above the doorway can still be read. It says that this was the tomb of the governor of Arabia, Sextius Florentinus, and it gives details of his previous career. Before being stationed in Arabia, he had been governor of southern Gaul. Before that, as a relatively young man, he had been one of the last legates commanding the famous Legion IX, the Ninth Hispana that perished in the mists of north Britain—or did it? The hints given by inscriptions may one day give us the true answer.

CHAPTER FOUR

New Knowledge—the Roman Army

It is time now to look at some of the discoveries that archaeologists have made and how these have thrown new light on our knowledge of the Romans. The contribution of archaeology is truly enormous, and the reason is that Roman writers and historians were for the most part concerned with recounting things and happenings that were *unusual*. They normally did not bother to describe in detail everyday life and the things of everyday life. It is the same with present-day writers: We have novelists and historians and journalists who write columns in newspapers and magazines on all topics under the sun. However, where would you easily find a clear and simple discussion of how a gas oven works or an account of a typical life in the day of a bus conductor? These things are taken for granted just as much now as their equivalents were in Roman times. Only archaeology can make good the loss. It is fair to say that archaeology has given us such a huge amount of new information about all aspects of Roman life that it would be impossible to give anything like a full survey unless the details of the actual discoveries were left out. Rather than do that, this chapter takes just one particular subject, the Roman army, and shows how new finds from all parts of the Roman Empire have enriched our knowledge.

In any study of Rome the army should take a special place. Its efficiency and discipline, not to mention its sheer size—a quarter of a million men—made it an object of fear and wonder to Rome's enemies. In a very real sense too, the Roman army has left its mark on the lands that Rome once ruled: the great network of Roman roads that linked the towns and cities of the Roman world. These were originally constructed by army engineers to serve as strategic highways, so that the Roman armies could move swiftly from one area of danger to another and so that supplies could be taken to the garrisons of the 65

66   The tombstone of Marcus Caelius.

frontier. These great highways have often survived to this day; true, they have sometimes changed out of recognition to suit the needs of modern traffic, but the arrow-straight directness of many roads betrays their Roman origin.

If one leaves aside the great strategic highways, archaeological evidence for the Roman army consists of three types. First, there are representations of the army in Roman art—particularly Roman sculpture. Here tombstones like that of Marcus Caelius are a rich source of information on such things as military dress and equipment. Caelius wears full parade uniform. His breastplate (*lorica*) was of hardened leather, moulded to the shape of the body and polished smooth. Below it can be seen the sort of skirt of overlapping strips of leather that protected the lower part of the body and the legs down to just above the knee. In his right hand Caelius holds a vine staff (*vitis*), which was no empty badge of office like the British officer's swagger stick but could be used on the backsides of the soldiers who were not "jumping to it" fast enough. Finally, falling over his left shoulder and swirling around under his arm to be caught in his left hand was his military cloak (*sagum*). Notice, too, the military decorations that he wears, equivalent to the modern soldier's medals. The thick and bushy oak wreath on his head was called the citizen's crown (*corona civica*). It has been called the Victoria Cross of the Roman army and was very rarely awarded and only to those who had saved the life of a comrade in battle. From each shoulder hang two miniature torques—the twisted neck ornament worn by Celtic warriors and adopted by the Romans as a military decoration, like the heavy bracelets on Caelius' wrists (*armillae*). On his chest there are six medallions (*phalerae*) attached to a sort of harness of leather. The central medallion has the head of a Gorgon on it—a terrible creature who occurs in classical legends. She was a monster with the face and body of a woman but with wings and twisting snakes instead of hair. If a Gorgon looked you in the eye, it had the unfortunate result of turning you into stone, and medallions with Gorgon heads were thought of as lucky charms that protected the wearer from his enemies. Poor Caelius—it did not help him much when the wild German hordes under Arminius ambushed three legions in the Teutoburg Forest (see page 63).

The sixty centurions in the legion were highly trained and

Tombstone of a centurion

The tombstone of
Caius Romanius.

highly paid professionals. Their families and friends could afford to pay for elaborate monuments of the sort provided for Caelius. But soldiers of lower rank could also have handsome tombstones, and this was true also of those men who were not Roman citizens at all but fought in Rome's auxiliary units.

The Roman army was divided into two classes of troops. There were first the thirty or so legions recruited solely from Roman citizens, and numbering between 5,000 and 6,000 men each. Alongside the legions fought smaller regiments, 500 or 1,000 strong, recruited from the native tribes that Rome had conquered. Most important were the cavalry units, for the legions were essentially infantry units. There were cavalry regiments of Gauls and Spaniards, men from the Danube provinces, regiments of Thracians, and regiments of Numidians. There were also other specialist troops such as slingers and archers, these last largely recruited in Syria. The auxiliary troops were paid less than the legionaries and served for longer periods, but there was never any lack of recruits because after their period of service the auxiliaries were given the coveted reward of becoming Roman citizens.

Some of the tombstones of the auxiliaries—especially the cavalrymen, who were slightly better paid than the infantry— were just as imposing as those of the legionaries and tell us just as much about dress and equipment. The example shown here belonged to a trooper in a cavalry regiment raised in the province of Noricum (Austria). Caius Romanius is shown triumphantly riding down a barbarian enemy. Notice how his feet hang free, for stirrups were not adopted in Europe until after the Roman period. This means that he could not charge an enemy in the way that cavalry have charged from the time of the medieval knights down to the nineteenth century, with the lance couched under the right arm. The troopers at the charge of the Light Brigade leaned forward in the saddle with their weight on the stirrups so that the shock of impact when their lance struck an enemy did not carry them clean out of the saddle. This is only possible with stirrups, so the Roman cavalry used their lances in a different way, stabbing downward at the enemy as they rode by. This is not so effective as the other way, but at least it meant that the troopers remained firmly in the saddle. Romanius holds the reins tightly in the left hand (behind his horse's head). His oblong shield is carried

Cavalry lance and spatha—the slashing sword of the auxiliary cavalryman.

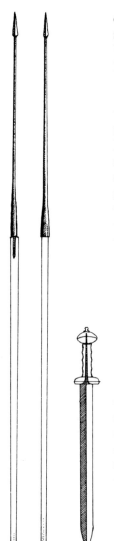

on the left arm by means of a couple of straps. Behind him a servant carries two spare lances, but if he dropped his lance in battle, he would have to rely on his long sword (*spatha*) that hangs by his right leg. With the spatha he could inflict a sweeping cut at his enemy as he rode by. This long type of cavalry sword contrasts with the short legionary *gladius* which was used for cut and thrust at close quarters, where there was no room to wield a larger weapon. The legionary soldier did not have a lance like the auxiliary cavalry trooper, but was equipped with a javelin (*pilum*). This had an iron point on the end of a long iron shaft fixed to the wooden handle. The iron shaft was deliberately not tempered (hardened by hammering); when the javelin struck an enemy's shield, the shaft would bend under the weight of the wooden handle and twist out of shape when he attempted to pull it out. This meant that it was non-returnable—the enemy could not hurl it back!

However, we learn most about the appearance of the Roman army, not from the tombstones but from two great monuments erected in Rome: Trajan's Column, built A.D. 113, and the Column of Marcus Aurelius, set up about sixty years later. Both columns are similar in general appearance, but the Column of Trajan shows much more detail, and we learn more from it. The Column of Trajan, as we are informed by an inscription on the base, was originally set up to show the height of the hillside that the Emperor Trajan ordered to be cut away so as to produce a level area on which he could begin a great scheme of new building. It was then decided to carve on the column scenes of Trajan's successful campaigns in Dacia (modern Rumania). The carvings were arranged in a continuous spiral strip that wound round and round the column. The work was carefully done, but the column is so high that one can only get a general impression looking at the scenes from the ground. To appreciate them properly, one should look at photographs or plaster casts.

One of the most interesting of all the scenes on the column shows the Roman field artillery in action. It also shows a Dacian prisoner being brought to the Emperor Trajan. Stationed behind him is a group of standard bearers. Notice, too, at the bottom left, the army medical corps at work. In the background can be seen the Roman "field guns," curious contraptions mounted on carts each drawn by a pair of horses. The soldiers

Two examples of the pilum (showing different methods of attaching to the wooden shaft) and the short legionary gladius.

Scene from Trajan's Column.

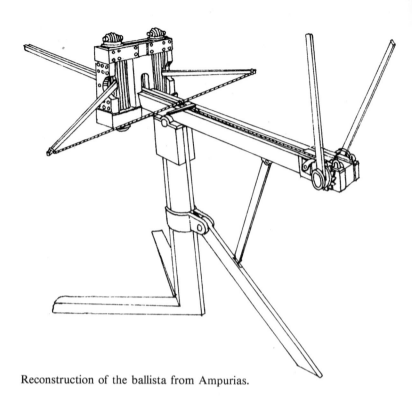

Reconstruction of the ballista from Ampurias.

operating the machines are protected by armour made out of strips
of metal, known in Latin as the *lorica segmentata*; they have
been shown much too large for the machines they are operating.
These machines, used for shooting heavy iron-tipped arrows,
were known as *ballistae*. The diagram above shows how the
ballista worked. The drawing is not just an imaginative reconstruction but based on finds of the actual iron parts of a Roman
catapult. They come from the site of Ampurias in Spain and are
the only remains of a ballista ever to have been found. How these
metal parts went together and what the wooden parts that have
not survived were like can be worked out by scholars with the aid
of the descriptions made by Greek and Roman technical writers.

Basically, a ballista like that from Ampurias worked on the
principle of a giant bow. The wooden bow itself (which in a
hand bow consists of a single piece of wood) is replaced by two
short arms. These are inserted in two twisted skeins of hair
rope. When the arms are pulled back by means of slipping a

72

hook over the bowstring and winding up a small windlass, the skeins are given an extra half twist. There is tremendous pressure on the wooden arms of the bow to spring forward and release the tension on the skeins, and as soon as the hook is released, they shoot forward. The bowstring immediately propels a short wooden arrow with a heavy iron point down the grooved wooden channel that acts as the barrel of the machine. The machine can be swung around and aimed to left or right, and the aim can be altered by raising or lowering the angle of the barrel.

The Ampurias catapult shows how archaeological discoveries can supplement the information we get from scenes on sculptured monuments like Trajan's Column. Such a find is especially exciting because even though iron is a very strong metal it rusts in the ground and only survives when conditions in the soil are exceptionally favourable. If even hard iron rusts away and disintegrates, it is hardly surprising that materials such as cloth or wood rarely survive. When they do, it is because the soil in which they have been buried is either extremely dry or else waterlogged. In these conditions dramatic discoveries can be made that immediately make the lively scenes on the column come even more alive for us.

Of all such finds one of the most thrilling is an actual Roman *A Roman flag* flag of the sort shown in some of the scenes on Trajan's Column. It comes from an unidentified site in Egypt and is now in the State Museum of Fine Arts, Moscow. The flag was dyed crimson. On it is a female figure standing on a globe. She is the Roman goddess of victory and holds a wreath in one hand and a palm branch in the other. The hem at the top of the flag shows that it was intended to be hung from a crossbar just like the flags shown on the column (see page 74).

Finds of Roman weapons and armour are surprisingly not particularly rare. An exception, however, is the lorica segmentata worn by the legionaries. This is because it was made out of thin iron strips that rust away only too easily. All that is generally found are the little bronze studs and fittings—the hinges and buckles that were used to fasten the armour together. Of the iron parts there remain usually only tantalizingly corroded lumps. Archaeologists puzzled over the pieces and attempted to make reconstructions. It was not until 1964 that the breakthrough came.

Roman banner (vexillum) from Egypt.

74

In the summer of 1964, archaeologists excavating at Corbridge, the Roman fort and supply base just south of Hadrian's Wall, made a remarkable discovery. They found, hidden under the charred floorboards of a Roman building, an iron-bound wooden box "in its final stages of disintegration." It had been hidden to avoid being found by barbarian raiders from Scotland who had swept southward destroying and pillaging Roman forts during a great rebellion about A.D. 100. In the box was found a miscellaneous collection of equipment—fragmentary wooden writing tablets, bundles of spearheads tied together with rope, four dozen black and white glass gaming counters, the remains of several cushions, and various pieces of scrap metal, iron tools and so on. One curious find was a mass of broken Roman window glass; the excavators argued from this that the fort may actually have been under attack when this curious assortment of objects was hurriedly bundled together and thrown in the chest for safekeeping. The really important finds in the chest were the dismantled pieces of several different suits of Roman body armour—the lorica segmentata—in an amazingly good state of preservation. They consist of great bands of steel that completely encircle the body. The bands slightly overlap one another and are fastened together by six leather straps. The straps, which are riveted to the different steel bands, run vertically from the top band to the bottom. This system of overlapping plates fastened together by straps allowed the bands to slide up and down over each other to a limited extent, thus following the movements of the body. This meant that legionaries were excellently protected but were not hindered in their movements. The upper part of the back and chest were protected by broader steel plates partly hinged together, partly connected by straps and buckles. The shoulders were protected by other overlapping strips, some of which were again fastened together by hinges.

Besides the lorica segmentata, the Roman legionary was protected by a large rectangular shield (*scutum*), curved so as to cover the front part of his body entirely. Like the lorica, it is well known from sculptured reliefs such as Trajan's Column. Like the lorica, it too has left little trace for archaeologists to discover. The lorica was at least made of iron, which has some chance of survival. The scutum was made of a sort of plywood, and wood is far more likely to perish and leave no

75

Lorica segmentata.

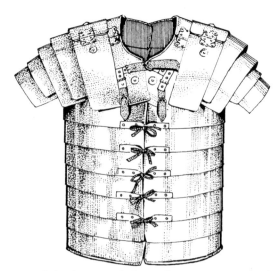

trace except for some of the bronze fittings that were attached to the shield. However, even wood can survive when conditions are right, and in the 1930's were found a whole series of objects made of perishable material like wood, cloth, and papyrus that are only rarely preserved. These finds, which come from the site of Dura on Rome's eastern frontiers, included the sole surviving example of a Roman legionary shield!

Dura-Europus and the Persian siege
The circumstances of this find are so exciting that the Corbridge discoveries seem insignificant in comparison. The city of Dura-Europus on the Euphrates River was one of the numerous Hellenistic towns that sprang up in the East after the conquests of Alexander the Great (356–323 B.C.). For several centuries it had lain beyond Rome's frontier with Parthia, till in A.D. 165 it was captured and occupied by the armies of Rome's philosopher-emperor Marcus Aurelius and became an important post on Rome's eastern frontier. However, the old Parthian empire was finally taken over by a new and vigorous dynasty of rulers who claimed descent from the ancient kings of Persia who had governed the land before the time of Alexander. The armies of this new "Persian" empire besieged and sacked Dura about A.D. 257.

Dura was rediscovered in 1921, when a certain Captain Murphy of the British army was digging military trenches among the ruins. Excavation followed, first of all by French archaeologists and then by an expedition sponsored by Yale University until stopped by the outbreak of the Second World War. Dura turned out to be an archaeological treasure house that its excavators claimed rivalled Pompeii in the interest of the discoveries and their state of preservation.

Like Pompeii, the end of Dura was dramatic. The Persians who were besieging the town were unable to take it by assault. Their problem was plain. They would have to cross the walls or destroy them, and they attempted to do both. They dug tunnels under the walls. The sides and roofs of the tunnels were supported with timber planking. The idea was to light fires of wood, tar and sulphur so that the wooden shoring would catch fire and collapse, and the walls which had been undermined would tumble in ruin. Besides digging three of these tunnels under the walls, the Persians also built a great ramp of earth against them in one place—this ramp still stands higher than the battlements of the city. This was a dodge that the Romans themselves had often used when attacking an enemy town. Attackers on the ramp would have a strong advantage over the defenders.

One Persian mine was dug near the main gate of the city. It ran up to and under the walls of one of the towers of the city wall and then branched out under the line of the wall itself. If all had gone according to plan, the whole tower and a large section of the city wall would have collapsed. But all did not go as planned. First, the defenders dug a countermine from inside the city, and a desperate battle took place between the Romans and the Persians in the dark tunnel under the walls of the city. The Romans were defeated and had to retreat back down their own tunnel. The bodies of eighteen of them were found in the countermine near its entrance. That they were Romans and not Persians is proved by the Roman coins they had with them—more than eighty of them. The latest of the coins dates to A.D. 256 and gives us an approximate date for the fall of the city. However, armour and weapons found with the bodies were not of the regular Roman types at all. They had jackets of mail, high helmets with mail flaps to protect the back of the neck, and bronze greaves—curved leg guards. Two of the warriors had great swords with pommels of jade and rock crystal. These were the bodies of Roman auxiliary troops. Some of the bodies, wrote the excavators, "were not completely

An underground battle

decomposed and still gave off a charnel odour." In one of the skulls a dried brain in good condition was found.

After this victory in the underground skirmish, the Persians set fire to the wooden supports of the countermine and blocked it off from their own with a wall of stone. The defenders dared not interfere again as the Persians quickly finished off their own mine and set fire to the supports. The collapse of the mine was only partly successful. Two of the walls of the tower sank into the great hollow excavated below its foundations. But, the walls did not fall because the Romans had heaped up a great mound of earth in front of them before the siege began as a protection against battering rams. However, the tower itself was virtually a ruin. Inside it were small chambers with wooden floors. The conflagration in the mine below somehow managed to penetrate to the tower above—the wooden beams caught and the floors collapsed. To the defenders it must have seemed —as indeed it was—the beginning of the end, but the doom that overtook their city has given them a certain immortality, just as the destruction of Pompeii has made that little town one of the most famous of Roman cities. *For the timbers of the wooden floors as they fell trapped a great hoard of armour and weapons stored in the tower's lowest chambers and preserved them from all decay for 1,700 years.*

It seems that the tower had been used as a depot for armour and weapons that needed repair, for although the objects were in almost perfect condition, most of them had been slightly damaged or broken at the time that the tower fell. The only exception to this were the arrows. Scores of arrows were found with shafts of cane or reed and feathered flights still in position. Many of these were charred, but they appeared to have been in usable condition. They were probably the ammunitions store for the archers on the tower. Among them was one heavy wooden arrow with a needle-sharp iron head and wooden shaft almost half a metre long. This would have been fired from a ballista— its sharp point specially designed to pierce the fish-scale armour of the Persians.

The armour awaiting repair in the tower included three sets of horse armour—horse "blankets" of coarse linen on which were sewn overlapping steel scales. There were also two pieces of armour to protect the thighs of cavalrymen; these were made of overlapping scales of leather boiled hard and were strapped

The ballista bolt from Dura with iron head and original wooden shaft.

onto the upper part of the leg. Finally, there was the legionary shield (see page 80).

The legionary shield—the only discovery of the great oblong scutum ever found—stood just over a metre high. It was made of a sort of plywood which gave strength, yet was comparatively light. In the centre a circular hole had been cut. This was covered by a projecting circular shield boss—the only part of the shield that was missing. Across the back of the shield from one side to the other was a strut of wood—it crossed the circular hole and so provided the user with a handgrip. The plywood was covered with leather, and there was a second covering of linen over the front. This had been painted red, and on this background different elaborate designs had been painted. One must imagine that the whole centre part of the shield was taken up by a square bronze plate with the circular shield boss in the middle. Such a plate was found in the Tyne River, it has engraved designs of eagles and standards on it and a bull—the symbol of Legion VIII, to which its owner, a certain Dubitatus, belonged. Around the place where this plate would have gone were painted fancy borders—a plait design, a sort of wreath pattern of leaves, and a simple "wave" pattern. Above this border were two winged Victories, like those on the flag from Egypt, crowning a legionary eagle with a wreath. Below is a rather mangy lion, perhaps the symbol of the legion, just as the bull was the symbol of Legion VIII on the Tyne shield boss. *The Dura shield*

So far in this chapter we have seen something of the arms and the equipment of the legions and the auxiliary soldiers. It is time to look at the great fortresses where the legions were stationed at intervals along the frontiers of the empire. Wherever possible, it was Roman policy to use natural barriers to mark the end of the Roman world and the beginning of the barbarian world beyond. The best frontiers of all, of course, were in the West, where the Atlantic Ocean meant that there *were* no barbarians outside who might pillage and raid and generally disturb the Roman peace. The deserts of North Africa were almost as effective. Elsewhere Rome had to rely on great rivers such as the Rhine and Danube in Europe and the Euphrates in the East or on artificial boundaries such as Hadrian's Wall in north Britain. Though such boundaries were clear enough—you couldn't exactly wander across the Rhine without noticing—a resolute enemy could always cross. This *Imperial frontiers*

A reconstruction of the Dura shield. The circular boss missing from the original has been restored.

80

is why the great frontier armies were concentrated in four military zones—Britain, the Rhineland, the Danube provinces, and Syria. It is in these areas that the legions—some thirty or so in number—were mainly based. Spain and North Africa required only one legion each.

Of these legionary bases, excavation has been carried out in something like a dozen. One of the most completely known is the fortress built by the famous governor Julius Agricola in Scotland, when it looked as if the whole island of Britain could have been finally conquered. The excavations at this site, Inchtuthil on the Tay, were carried out by Sir Ian Richmond from 1952 to 1965. This fortress was defended by a great wall of stone, but the buildings inside were built out of less durable materials: timber frames on which hurdles were woven, which were then covered over with mud and plastered. Such buildings leave little trace except for the trenches in which the foundation timbers—sleeper beams—have been laid. These, however, could be accurately planned, and the ground plan of the whole fortress recovered. Inchtuthil is particularly interesting because the Roman government decided that it could not spare the troops to finish off Agricola's conquests in Scotland and therefore abandoned the site. This means that we have the original layout of the fortress just as it was first designed by the legionary architects. There are no confusing later additions to the plan to sort out, no building periods to establish.

A Roman fortress in Scotland

Important as Inchtuthil is to the archaeologists and to military historians studying the Roman army, a visit to the site would be something of a disappointment, as there is now nothing left to see above ground, and this is true of most of the other legionary fortresses. An exception is the site of Lambaesis in Algeria. This was the base of Legion III Augusta throughout the second and third centuries A.D. In some ways Lambaesis is a typical legionary fortress, although it must be admitted that in other respects it is unusual. This is because it was largely remodelled during the third century A.D. after an earthquake. These third century additions are of great interest in themselves, and the whole fortress and the surrounding area are worth describing in some detail.

The fortress of Legion III Augusta

Lambaesis, fortress of the Third Augusta, lies at the foot of the Aurès Mountains in the Roman province of Numidia. The tradition of the military associations with the area lingers on in

81

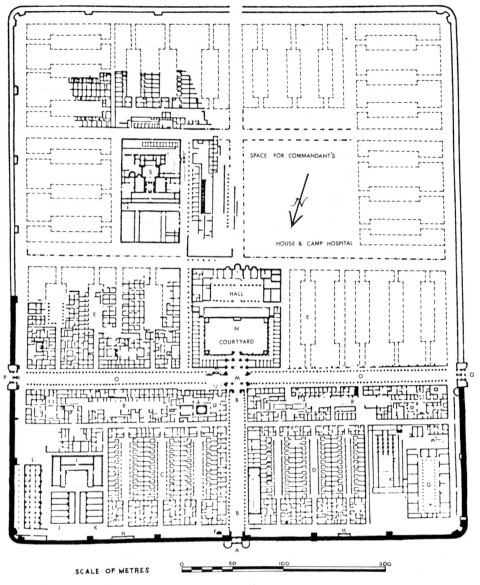

Plan of Lambaesis, the great legionary base in Algeria (*the buildings marked with letters are referred to in text*).

the Arab name for the mountains that overlook the site—the Djebel Askar, the Mountains of the Soldier. It was visited several times by travellers in the nineteenth century, who recorded the appearance of its main surviving building, the so-called Praetorium, more than a century ago. Unfortunately in the middle of the nineteenth century the French authorities built a detention centre in one corner of the site. This meant that part of the plan of the fortress was irretrievably lost beneath the new buildings, while some Roman buildings that were still standing were robbed of their stone to make the new prison. However, it was still possible to excavate great areas of the fortress. In fact, because all legionary fortresses have a fairly similar plan, it is even possible to attempt a reconstruction of the complete layout.

The fortress was entered from the north through a double archway flanked by two great D-shaped towers (A on the plan). This main entrance would have been known to the legionaries as the Praetorian Gate—the *Porta Praetoria*—not only here at Lambaesis, but at all other forts and fortresses throughout the empire. The Romans had special names for the main buildings in their forts, for the gates, and even for the streets, and it is often convenient to use these names when we talk about their remains today. Passing through the Porta Praetoria, then, the visitor now, as in Roman times, is confronted by a broad well-paved road, flanked by colonnades, the Praetorian Way (*Via Praetoria*, BB). *The Praetorian Gate*

On either side of the Via Praetoria to left and right were groups of barrack blocks (C and D) where the soldiers lived— six barracks to the left and six to the right. The barracks were arranged so as to face one another across a narrow roadway. These barrack blocks are of great interest. They conform to a single plan. There is a range of thirteen small rooms entered by a narrow passage which skirts a small subsidiary annexe, where arms and equipment could be stored. Three of these suites of paired room and annexe were probably set aside for the non-commissioned officers, but the other ten each housed a group of eight men, a *contubernium*. This word refers, literally, to a small group of people who shared the same hut or tent. In the British army the contubernium would correspond to the section. There were therefore ten sections of 8 men in each barrack block—in other words, just 80 men. They were known *The barracks* as a century (*centuria*) and were commanded by a centurion. The centurion was a tough long-service officer who had *his* quarters at the end of the barrack block, nearest the walls of the fortress. If there was any trouble, he would be the first to hear about it. In front of each barrack block was a colonnade—a veranda, in fact, that ran the whole length of the building. There the soldiers could drink and play dice in the shade.

Each group of six barracks housed a cohort, some 480 men. On the plan you will see that ten groups of barracks have been either discovered or restored, for there were ten cohorts in the legion. There are, however, extra barracks for the first cohort (E on the plan) because this was always kept at double strength. The cohorts of 480 men each plus extra for the first cohort give the legion a total strength of something more than 5,000 men.

Just inside the Porta Praetoria on the left was a fountain (F)—handily placed to fill your water skins if you were about to leave on patrol or to slake your thirst if you were returning from desert reconnaissance. The only other thing between the barrack blocks and the fortress walls were two latrines (H), one for each cohort. Otherwise, this whole area was kept free, partly to avoid fire risk if the desert raiders should attack with fire arrows, partly to allow the legionaries quick access to the walls and the ballistae mounted at intervals along them on great masonry platforms.

Behind the barracks to east and west were other buildings whose functions are not all clear. To the west were two large buildings between the barrack blocks and the fortress wall. One (G) had two great rows of columns supporting the roof of a large hall and large rooms opening off it. The excavators thought it was the camp hospital. Perhaps it was really the great hangar-like workshop where the legionary armourers and engineers repaired anything from the hinge on a lorica segmentata to a broken ballista.

Between the other set of barracks and the fortress wall were four buildings (I, J, and K). These were probably store buildings of some kind. Beyond, a building (L) was almost certainly a stable block. It had a central corridor with a series of rooms opening off it. There are internal buttresses on the walls of these rooms against which the wooden partitions of the stalls would have been fixed.

84

The "Praetorium" at Lambaesis as it appeared in the nineteenth century. The Via Praetoria entered the large entrance on the left, and the Via Principalis the large blocked entrance on the right.

At the far end of the Via Praetoria is an imposing building (M). Looking at it from the Praetorian Gate, one sees spanning the Via Praetoria a huge archway large enough for wheeled vehicles to pass through. There are smaller arched openings for pedestrians at each side. Above the central arch is the great window of a large upper chamber whose wooden floor has long since rotted. This imposing building has been known as the Praetorium since the nineteenth century. It is misleading because the praetorium was the official name for the commanding officer's quarters, and this building is nothing of the sort. It is, in fact, no more than a monumental entrance hall to the building that lies on its far side, the most important in the whole fort—the headquarters building, or *Principia* (N). A very inconvenient entrance porch, one might think the so-called Praetorium, for it has been built just at the intersection of two of the principal roadways of the fort, the Via Praetoria (BB)

The "Praetorium"

85

and the *Via Principalis* (OO), which make a T junction with it just in front of the headquarters building. But there were other great archways for vehicles and people on foot on both sides of the Praetorium, so that traffic could pass freely through the building. The Praetorium was built, as an inscription shows, after a great earthquake, A.D. 267, which caused much damage to the fortress, and it was not an original part of the design.

The headquarters building

The Praetorium gave access to the headquarters building (Principia, N). This was divided into four parts. First came a great paved courtyard surrounded by one of those colonnades that seem to be such a regular feature of the fortress. Opening off this colonnade were a series of rooms or offices. Many of them were used for armaments stores, as inscriptions which were once let into the wall above the doorways show. In one room 6,000 baked clay slingstones and another 300 stone ones were found. The sling was not a regular weapon of the legionary soldiers, and these finds must come from a time late in the fortress' history when the old methods were changing. On the far side of the courtyard was a low terrace reached by two steps. From the front of this a platform projected out into the courtyard. Was this the platform from which the commanding officer, with his officers grouped behind him, addressed sections of the legion under his command? Behind this terrace and about the height of a man above it was a great aisled hall, its roof supported on two rows of columns. In front of the second row of columns stood the bases of statues of different emperors, paid for, as inscriptions on them show, by the senior centurions in the legion.

Shrine of the standards

Finally, behind the aisled hall came a row of small rooms and offices. Some of these were square chambers, but in others the far wall has been taken down and a curved wall built in its place, forming an apse. The central room had one of these apses, as well as the square base for an altar. Below the floor were a series of underground vaults. This was the most important part of the whole headquarters building, for there behind the altar stood the eagle of the legion and the other legionary standards. There at the altar the legionaries could make sacrifices to the very spirit of the legion in which they served—embodied in the great legionary standard. The eagle glared through the smoke of burned offerings on the altar out through the open doorway of the shrine and across the vaulted

86

hall, through its entrance straight on across the paved court-yard and the great arched portals of the Praetorium down the Via Praetoria to the Praetorian Gate in the far distance. There the eagle received the offerings of the soldiers, from the newest recruit to the commanding officer, and waited for a time when it should be taken from its resting place and lead the legion down the Praetorian Way and out to war.

In the vaulted chambers below the shrine great sacks of coin were stored—the savings of the soldiers compulsorily deducted from their pay. There were eleven sacks in all—one for the savings of each cohort, and one, the eleventh, to pay for the funeral expenses of those who should die in battle. To the left and right of the shrine were other apsed rooms. These were the meeting places for soldiers' clubs. Many of the different grades of soldiers in the legion had their own special club or associa-tion and their own meeting place with its own private "chapel." Such an organization and the place where it met was known as a schola—our word "school" is derived from it.

Along the front of the Principia ran the Via Principalis, like the Via Praetoria, a well-paved colonnaded roadway. The Via Principalis connected two of the main gates of the fortress (P and Q). These gates were similar to the Praetorian Gate (A), although the flanking towers were of a somewhat different design.

North of the Via Principalis and running from one end to the other was a series of houses (R). These take the form of a court-yard around which are grouped the different rooms. In the centres of the courtyards were ornamental pools and tanks. These houses belonged to the six tribunes, who were some of the most important officers in the legion.

Behind the Principia were baths (S). The floors of the different *The baths* rooms, as is usual, were built resting on a whole series of small rectangular brick pillars in such a way that hot air heated in a furnace room could pass underneath them. Such an under-floor heating system is known as a hypocaust, from a Greek word meaning "burning beneath." Once the hot air had circulated underneath the floors it passed up rectangular clay pipes sunk in the thickness of the wall to find its way out from vents under the eaves. This meant that the walls, like the floors, were heated, too, and that moisture from the hot baths would not condense on the walls as it would have done if they had not 87

The mosaic from the legionary baths. On the left is Luna, the moon goddess. On the right is Sol, the sun god.

been heated. The baths were of different temperatures, and the bather first plunged into water of moderate heat and then slowly worked up till he entered baths where the temperature was only just bearable. The heat caused the pores to open, and the bather "sweated out" all the grime and dirt that his body had picked up. It is easy to imagine the soldiers enjoying the hot water after coming back from a week's patrol in the desert, singing and shouting as they splashed around in the hot water. The final stage was a quick dip in an ice-cold plunge bath. This both refreshed the bather and helped close the pores.

The baths were the camp's social centre, where the soldiers relaxed and generally had a good time. At Lambaesis the building was an impressive one, with painted wall plaster that imitated panels of polished marble and elaborate mosaics. One of the pavements had represented the head of the sun-god Sol, with rays coming from it, and the head of the moon-goddess Luna complete with appropriate symbols—a crescent and a torch. The African recruits of Legion III Augusta will have known them by their Carthaginian names, Baal and Tanit.

This concludes our description of the great fortress of Lambaesis, one of the most exciting sites in the whole empire. It is well to remember that the fortress did not stand isolated, alone in the desert. From the Eastern Gate ran a road called

88

the Via Septimiana, after the third-century Emperor Septimius Severus, who ordered it to be paved in stone. The Via Septimiana ran to a nearby town. On its way the road passed an amphitheatre, a great oval building with stepped seats that looked downward on a sort of circus ring. Amphitheatres were regularly built near legionary fortresses—so that the legionaries could watch not only gladiatorial duels and beast shows, but also, and more important, demonstrations of arms drill and complicated military manoeuvres.

The presence of a town near a legionary fortress is again typical. All large military camps, then as now, attract the presence of civilians who realize that soldiers, who are regularly paid, have money to spend and who are only too happy to help them spend it. Lambaesis, the town, was a fine place that you entered and left by great triumphal arches built in honour of Septimius Severus. *The town of Lambaesis*

From the eastern gate of the fort a second road ran—under yet a third triumphal arch built in honour of the Emperor Commodus. It led to the famous city of Thamugadi, or Timgad (see Chapter 5).

Several roads left the Porta Praetoria. One led to the so-called camp of the auxiliaries slightly less than two kilometres away. This was about half the size of the legionary fortress and has proved a great puzzle to archaeologists. Perhaps it was not a camp at all but a parade ground. In the centre was a paved area where a column on a base once stood. The base was inscribed with the text of a long speech made by the Emperor Hadrian to the men of the Third Augusta and the soldiers in several auxiliary regiments when he visited Lambaesis A.D. 128 and watched the troops on manoeuvres. The inscription shows how impressed the emperor was with the discipline and skill of the troops on that hot July day more than 1,800 years ago. "If there had been anything amiss, I would have noticed it; if anything had been obviously wrong, I would point it out. But you pleased me uniformly throughout the whole exercise. . . ." *Hadrian inspects the Legion*

In this chapter one of the great legionary fortresses has been described in detail. The auxiliary forts were, of course, much smaller in size, being intended for units only 500 or 1,000 strong; but for all that they were remarkably like the legionary bases—only in miniature. Many of the best-preserved auxiliary 89 forts are in Britain, as anyone who has ever visited the site of Housesteads or Chesters on Hadrian's Wall will know. But complete or nearly complete plans of forts have been recovered on other frontiers, for example, Valkenburg in Holland and recently Künzing in southern Germany.

Lambaesis as it looks today.

CHAPTER FIVE

Survey of the Roman Empire

All the countries that border the Mediterranean are rich in the remains of Rome's flourishing empire, from Spain in the West to Syria in the East. It would be impossible in a short book to do justice to even a fraction of the famous sites that reward the archaeological tourist who is "looking for Rome" in these countries. So this chapter will have to be selective. It is not necessarily concerned with the best-preserved monuments, but first and foremost with those that are in some ways typical of the empire.

In Chapter 2 we saw something of one of the cities in the *Cities of* eastern part of the empire. In some ways Knidos is typical of *the East* the cities of the Greek East, though there are many variations in detail. The most exciting cities in the East are undoubtedly the great caravan cities of the eastern provinces, in Syria, Jordan, and Lebanon: Palmyra in a great ocean of desert, or Baalbeck at the foot of the mountains of Lebanon, or Petra literally cut out of the living rock, or Jerash nestling in the hills of Jordan. These are sites that stir the imagination. They must always have been exciting places, with the constant coming and going of traders and camel caravans. Each of these cities is highly individual, and one could write a book about any one of them.

The same is true of the many cities of the western empire, *New cities* too. But here there was one important difference. In the West *in the West* civilization had not such deep roots. In many areas such as large tracts of North Africa, Spain, and Gaul—and especially far-off Britain—there were no true cities before the Romans came, only a few colonies of Greeks and Carthaginians on the North African coasts and in southern France and Spain. In the areas where there were no cities, Rome came not only as a conqueror but as a bringer of civilization. She created new towns. Some of these were settlements for the local inhabitants; some 91 were specially built for retired legionaries in good farming country. There the veterans could settle down to a comfortable retirement. Such towns were called colonies. A Roman colony (*colonia*) was, however, different from a colony in our sense of the word. It was not a large territory lying overseas to which colonists emigrated or were sent. It was simply a single town of veterans set down in the middle of a conquered area—one of the provinces of the Roman Empire.

*Roman
"colonies"
provide a
model*

Of all the towns in the West, the Roman colonies were the most Romanized of all. The other towns that sprang up in the provinces were largely copies of the Roman colonies. This was true of both their physical appearance and the sort of life that went on within their walls. Both Roman colonies and the other towns, at any rate the larger ones, were run by town councils, consisting of a hundred town councillors, or decurions. The town councils were the real power in running local affairs. But there were also magistrates who were elected by the ordinary citizens. Two judicial magistrates who presided over the local lawcourts, called duoviri, were chief among these, just as the two consuls at Rome were the chief magistrates in the capital of the Roman Empire. Then there were two aediles who were in charge of public works—they were assisted by a small number of public slaves who saw that the streets were kept clean and that temples and other public buildings were kept in repair. Finally, there were often two further officials called quaestors who were in charge of the financial affairs of the little towns.

We know of the existence of many of these magistrates in all parts of the western empire from the numerous inscriptions that they set up on buildings whose cost they paid for or from inscriptions cut on the bases of statues erected in their honour by the grateful townsfolk. There were duoviri in Pompeii, just as there were duoviri in towns like Cirencester or Gloucester in Britain. We know, too, a vast amount about the duties and obligations of these magistrates and the laws by which the towns were run from a series of inscribed bronze tablets found at different sites in Spain—one of them a Roman colony founded by Julius Caesar called Urso between Granada and Seville.

If we want, therefore, to look at a typical town in the western empire, it would make sense to look at a Roman colony. There

are two Roman colonies that spring to mind. One everyone
has heard of. It is Pompeii—whose full name was Colonia
Veneria Cornelia. Pompeii, overwhelmed by the great eruption
of A.D. 79, is a unique site: the objects of everyday life found in
the houses of the ruined town give the most vivid glimpse
imaginable into the life of the people who lived there almost
2,000 years ago. The archaeological tourist should visit Pompeii
not once, but several times, for the first visit is often a disappointment. There is so *much* of Pompeii, and it is so *hot*.
But after two or three visits the town begins to grow on you.
You begin to know Pompeii as you know a modern town. After
a while you can start to dispense with the map of the city, and
you begin to get a feel for the plan of the place. You know
that if you cut across in a certain direction, you will come out
at the baths or the forum or the theatre. Yet Pompeii is much
older than the sort of newly founded cities that sprang up in
the provinces, and as such it is not typical. In the old part of
the town there are narrow streets and cobbled alleyways that
would not look at all in place in the newly created cities with
their rigidly constructed grid of streets, intersecting at right
angles like the squares on a chessboard. And, too, there are
many good books in English on Pompeii, so that it is easy to
find out about the city and the people who lived there.

The second Roman colony is much more typical of the new
towns in the West, and although not so well preserved as
Pompeii, it gives a true picture of the "ordinary" provincial
town. This is Timgad in Algeria—or, to give it its full name,
Colonia Marciana Trajana Thamugadi. Built by the Emperor
Trajan (A.D. 98–117), it was called after both himself and his
sister Marciana. In only one respect is Timgad abnormal. Unlike Pompeii and most towns in the western empire, though not
in the East, Timgad had no amphitheatre.

Timgad lies some 20 kilometres east of Lambaesis on the
high plateau which separates the two ranges of the Atlas
Mountains. It is a fertile spot, comparatively well watered and
one where the veterans of Legion III Augusta could grow two
of the most important crops of the ancient world—grain and
olives. The corn was, of course, used for making bread, while
the olives were crushed in great presses so as to give oil. The
oil was used both for lamps and for cooking. The presses consisted of a great beam pivoted between two uprights at one end

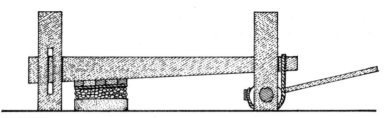

Press to crush olives. It worked on the principle of a giant nutcracker.

and winched down by a sort of windlass at the other. This beam crushed the olives, which were placed on a great stone block, and forced out the oil. Such presses have been found in the area surrounding Timgad and, when brigands made life outside the walls of the town less secure, were also built in the town. In far-off Britain, for just the same reasons, ovens used for drying corn that had been harvested damp were found built *inside* the town of Verulamium (modern St. Albans).

Frontier town   Although Timgad was favourably placed from an agricultural point of view, the spot may not have been chosen with such things in mind. The site of the town was perhaps originally occupied by a legionary base—the predecessor of Lambaesis, in fact. The garrison would have kept a wary eye on the mountains to the south in which Numidian rebels lurked. They were never defeated, although Roman roads encircled the mountains and Roman forts were strung out along the roads. When the legion moved on westward to Lambaesis, a colony was founded on the old site. There veterans from Lambaesis could lead a life of retirement not far from the base that had been their home for so many years and in the country that they had come to know and love. At Timgad they would not have entirely ceased to be soldiers, for in an emergency the town militia could always have sallied out to meet and drive back invaders. So it may have been for some 400 years, but about A.D. 500 raiders sacked the town. The generals of the Emperor Justinian reoccupied the town again within 50 years and built a great fort outside it to the north, but when Roman power in Africa finally fell, the site became deserted. It was rediscovered 94   by the English traveller Bruce in 1765 (see page 19) and has been excavated by the French from the end of the nineteenth century onward. Hand in hand with the work of excavation has gone a limited amount of reconstruction—walls have been consolidated and fallen columns raised so that now Timgad is one of the show places of Roman North Africa.

The most striking thing about Timgad is its layout. The streets form a rigid chessboard-pattern dividing up the building blocks. Some of these were taken up with public buildings—baths, a theatre like the one at Knidos and even a public library. At the centre of the town was the main square (*forum*) with the town hall at one end and temples and the council chamber (*curia*) at the other. The streets were adorned with fountains and statues and the main ones were flanked with colonnades so that you could walk from one end of the town to the other in the shade. In its heyday Timgad must have been pleasant enough. A city of comfortable houses with shaded little gardens and courts, of temples, and always a couple of blocks away a bathhouse where you could freshen up and idle away a hot afternoon. It was not the sort of place to attract tourists in ancient times—although the only spot of life to be had for miles around if you were unfortunate enough to be one of the legionaries serving in the Third Augusta at Lambaesis.

If the ancient tourist might have been disappointed, his modern equivalent may also feel a touch of disappointment, too. Timgad is the most complete example of a city of its type anywhere in the Roman Empire. However, apart from the great Arch of Trajan, its ruins are on the whole not very impressive. It stands in the desert like a petrified forest of columns—all the roofs are lacking, and it is not easy to picture the ruins as real buildings. In one respect, too, Timgad is unusual as far as Roman colonies are concerned; it apparently lacked an amphitheatre in which gladiatorial games and beast shows were held. If an archaeological tourist would like to see an amphitheatre, he must look elsewhere.

The habit of watching wild beasts and gladiators fighting, often to the death, was peculiarly Roman and reflects a very unpleasant side of the Roman character. The scale of these beast shows was enormous. The Emperor Augustus, usually considered a most humane and civilized person, a man who made a virtue of living simply and who was worshipped by the people of the empire for having given them the gift of peace

Gladiatorial and beast shows

after the civil wars, boasted in the list of his achievements set up by his tomb (see page 61) that in Rome he put on twenty-six shows in which wild beasts from Africa were hunted. In these shows about 3,500 animals were killed. In the eight gladiatorial games that he financed in his own name or on behalf of his sons and grandsons, some 10,000 gladiators fought, though we do not know how many of these fought to the death. Finally, he boasts that he had an artificial lake excavated in which he held a mock sea fight between thirty warships with countless smaller ships. On board were 3,000 fighting men. Subsequent emperors increased the scale of such spectacles, which became popular not only at Rome, but all over the western empire. In the eastern part of the empire, however, a more civilized attitude toward such cruel sports prevailed. The Greeks were much more interested in music and drama, athletics, and chariot races. A city like Knidos had two theatres and two small odea for musical performances and could well have had a stadium for horse races. Only when there were Roman colonies in the Greek East, for example, at Cyzicus near Troy, does one find an amphitheatre.

In the West almost any city of any size had its amphitheatre, and many of these survive—for example, at Verona in north Italy, Pula in Yugoslavia, or in some number in the south of France and in Spain. In Spain, Roman amphitheatres are still used for bullfights, and the same is true of southern France, although there the bullfights are not such gory affairs. The most famous amphitheatre in the Roman world is, of course, the Colosseum in Rome—or as the Romans themselves called it, the Flavian Amphitheatre. It was built by the Roman Emperor Vespasian (reigned A.D. 70–79) and his son Titus (emperor from A.D. 79 to 81). This huge building, the ancestor of our modern circus rings and sports stadiums, is estimated to have been able to hold 87,000 spectators. At its opening no less than 5,000 animals were slaughtered! Under the amphitheatre arena were subterranean chambers from which animals could be pulled up in cages by a system of pulleys so that they seemed suddenly to appear as if from nowhere. The Colosseum, too, could be

Timgad, a petrified forest of columns, with the arch of Trajan in the foreground and the theatre in the background.

flooded and mock naval battles held there, to the delight of thousands of spectators.

Cities of Provence   One does not have to go as far even as Rome to see excellent examples of this sort of building. Some of the best-preserved amphitheatres are to be found in the south of France. This is the area that the Romans called Provincia Narbonensis after one of their earliest military colonies, Narbo Martius, modern Narbonne. Narbonensis is a bit of a mouthful, and the area gradually came to be known simply as the Province, and so today we call the south of France by the old name, Provence. It was one of the most thoroughly Romanized areas of the empire, full of flourishing towns and cities, and although none of the larger ones survives in its entirety like Timgad or Pompeii, in many can still be seen fine buildings as well preserved as any in the Roman Empire. The triumphal arch and theatre at Orange, for example, are two of the best-preserved monuments of their type to be found anywhere. As far as amphitheatres are concerned, those in two cities in particular stand out, Nîmes and Arles. Both were Roman colonies, and as was usual with Roman colonies their official names were long and rather pompous. Nîmes, not a true colony, was called by the shorter name, Colonia Augusta Nemausus, while Arles was known as Colonia Julia Paterna Sextanorum Arelatensium, or Arelate for short. *Sextanorum* means "of the men of the sixth" and refers to soldiers of Legion VI who were settled there just as soldiers of the Third were settled at Timgad.

Amphitheatres at Nîmes and Arles   The general plan and siting of the amphitheatres at these two towns were so similar that archaeologists believe that they must date probably to more or less the same period (perhaps the middle of the first century A.D.) and were the work of the same architect, or at least that one amphitheatre copies the design of the other. Both are placed inside the town, which is by no means always the case, and both later, in the medieval period, became fortresses. At Arles, some of the towers that were built onto the Roman structure still survive. Their general plan resembles that of all amphitheatres—a great oval arena surrounded by tier upon tier of seats. This layout recalls the word "amphitheatre" itself which means double theatre, because in the ordinary theatre the seats of the cavea formed a simple semicircle, while in the amphitheatre they occupied both sides of the arena.

98

View of the outside of the amphitheatre at Nîmes.

Spectators who wanted to reach the seats of the cavea could enter any of the arched entrances at ground level. Behind the wall with its arcades lay a series of galleries which ran all the way round the amphitheatre and on which the seating was constructed. These galleries were connected by passages and staircases and so enabled the audience to arrive at any part of the auditorium with the minimum of confusion. Their presence also meant an immense saving in the amount of material used to support the seats of the cavea. The passages through which the audience passed out onto the stepped seats were known as vomitoria. It has been estimated that the Nîmes amphitheatre could have held some 17,000 spectators—a huge number but still some 70,000 less than the Colosseum! A clever device ensured that this vast audience could leave after a performance without getting jammed tight in the passageways. The higher one went, the narrower were the staircases, so that the flow of people coming down was always regulated, and there was always room on the wider lower staircases to take the ever-increasing numbers.

The cavea

The seats were divided into three main zones. Naturally the best seats were the lowest. In front of these three zones were four rows of seats reserved for local notables, particularly the members of the town council, the magistrates, and the priests. There, too, were special seats for members of influential trade guilds, particularly the guilds of bargemen who managed the

99

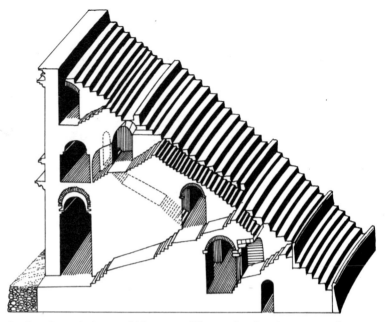

Section through the amphitheatre at Nîmes, showing the system of staircases and galleries that gave access to the auditorium.

important transportation businesses on the great inland waterways of southern France. At Arles, too, the *diffusores olearii*—the guild of olive oil merchants—had "reserved seats" at the front of the cavea. These seats were somewhat wider to accommodate the more ample proportions of the successful businessmen and town councillors. All alike were protected from the hot Provençal sun by a great awning—the velum. The sockets for the supporting poles for this survive cut in massive stones which project from the back wall of the cavea.

The arena   The arena was constructed at a considerably lower level than the lowest seats, from which it was separated by a high wall; it was all very well having a front seat provided you didn't have to share it with a lion! At Arles the present level of the arena floor appears to be much lower than necessary; this is because the arena floor has gone. It would have been raised well above the present ground level, leaving a great subterranean area below. There beasts could be kept, and from there, just as in the Colosseum, they could be raised by machinery at appropriate moments. Something similar existed at Nîmes, where two

100

wide subterranean passageways have been found under the level of the arena, crossing each other at right angles in the centre.

Such were the two great amphitheatres at Nîmes and Arles. It is reassuring to note that these great monuments, symbols of one of the worst aspects of Roman civilization, are not the only great buildings to survive in these two cities. Arles has a fine theatre, and at Nîmes, among other monuments, is the so-called Temple of Diana, a building with niches in its wall and a vaulted roof, which still survives. It has been suggested that it may have been a library. But at Nîmes one building stands out above all others. It is perhaps the best-preserved and most perfect of all temples in the Roman world, the justly famed Maison Carrée.

It is easy to see how the building, which was used as a church in the Middle Ages, got its name, for Maison Carrée simply means "square house," and the temple has a perfectly rectangular plan. It is known that the Maison Carrée was set

Maison Carrée

The Maison Carrée at Nîmes. The most perfect of all Roman temples.

in an open space surrounded by a colonnade. This could have been either a special temple courtyard, or perhaps was just one end of the central main square of Nîmes—the forum.

The Maison Carrée has been built like most Roman temples on a high platform or podium and is approached by a flight of steps at the front end—one of the short ends of the oblong. Six fluted columns with Corinthian capitals here support a stone beam, known to architects as the architrave. Above this comes the frieze, decorated with a beautiful floral scroll pattern along the sides of the temple but plain in front. Finally, above the frieze, comes the cornice, the part that sticks out below the roof, forming the eaves of the building. At the front the cornice frames a triangular space known as the pediment. Behind the porch of the temple, which is three columns deep, comes the temple proper—the shrine itself, a rectangular room, known again technically as the cella. At the far end of the cella was normally placed a statue of the god or goddess to whom the temple was dedicated. The side walls of the cella have half columns attached to them, or engaged columns, as they are usually known. Terms like architrave and cornice, podium and cella are a little difficult to remember at first, but any temple of classical form will be made up of these architectural parts, and there are really no other words for them.

One of the important things about the Maison Carrée, apart from its miraculous state of preservation, is that we know the precise date at which it was built 20–19 B.C. We learn this from an inscription in bronze letters which were originally attached to the frieze just below the pediment. The bronze letters have long since been removed and melted down, but scholars who have carefully recorded the positions of the holes into which the bronze pegs that held the inscription in place were let have been able to tell what it once said. There is perhaps no temple standing that rivals it in its pure and restrained classical Roman style, a style that had its finest flowering during the reign of Rome's first emperor, Augustus.

Pont du Gard   In the neighbourhood of Nîmes there is one further outstanding Roman monument that it would be hard to pass over in silence. This is the great aqueduct that originally brought water a total of 50 kilometres to the Roman city—the famous Pont du Gard. In the judgment of Lady Brogan, the foremost British

102   authority on Roman Gaul, this is the most beautiful of all the

The Pont du Gard—part of the great aqueduct that brought a water supply to Nîmes—from a nineteenth-century engraving.

monuments of this rich area. No Roman city was complete without its baths and its fountains—or for that matter its public lavatories—and we have seen how well provided Timgad was in these amenities. To supply the water for them, it was necessary to bring it by covered pipelines from rivers or springs that lay at a higher level than the town that they were supplying—unless pumps were to be used. To find such a source often meant going a considerable distance from the town; then if valleys and rivers lay in the way, the pipeline had to make a detour, or the Roman engineers had to carry it across a bridge over the obstacle. A third possibility was to enclose the pipeline in thick concrete and carry it down a valley and up the other side; provided that there was an overall drop in level, the water would still flow on the principle of an inverted siphon. The Roman engineers used a great aqueduct consisting of three superimposed series of arches 48 meters high to carry the Nîmes water supply over the Gardon River. In the eighteenth   103 century a series of additional arches were built against the lowest arches of the aqueduct to carry a road across the river. This is the most impressive, but by no means the only, bridge that carries the Nîmes aqueduct. The water also passes through a number of tunnels on its way to Colonia Augusta Nemausus.

Baths and aqueducts   As with temples, so too with aqueducts, impressive examples are to be found in all parts of the Roman world, including Rome itself. Rome required a vast amount of water, for besides having the greatest amphitheatre it also possessed some of the greatest bath buildings. The Baths of Diocletian (reigned A.D. 284–305) now house the national museum of archaeological antiquities, while the Baths of Caracalla (reigned A.D. 211–217) serve as the setting for opera. The only time that I watched a performance there I fell asleep during a performance of *Lohengrin* (it was after a hard day's work on an excavation near Naples) and only woke up as live horses came onto the stage!

However, there is no country more than Spain that one thinks of in connection with aqueducts. Here the aqueducts at

The bridge at Alcántara in Spain—still in use after eighteen centuries.

Tarragona, just west of Barcelona, and at Segovia are outstanding. The Segovia aqueduct, 16 kilometres long, is not so high as the Pont du Gard but is in its own way just as impressive. The granite blocks of which it is built are put together without mortar, and after almost 2,000 years it still carries water to the town as it did in Roman times.

Nor must one forget the fact that Spain is famous for one of the best known of Roman road bridges, the great bridge over the Tagus river at Alcántara, built A.D. 106. Just as the Pont du Gard has been reckoned the most beautiful of all the monuments of Roman Gaul, so the Alcántara bridge has been claimed as the finest monument in Spain. It still carries the modern roadway which passes under an archway erected in honour of Trajan in the very centre of the bridge. . . . *The later empire*

This brief survey of the empire started with Timgad, typical of the new towns that sprang up under the Roman Empire in the West, and then concentrated on a few of the best-preserved and most typical Roman buildings and engineering works known—the amphitheatres, temples, and bridges. All these works belong to the first two centuries A.D., the heyday of the empire; nothing has been said of the remains of the fourth century A.D.: the great fortress of Diocletian at Split on the Dalmatian coast of Yugoslavia or the city of Trier on the Moselle. Trier is a city that acted as one of the fourth-century capitals of the Roman Empire; it has one of the most famous of all Roman gates, the so-called Porta Nigra. Besides the Porta Nigra, Trier boasts the remains of massive late-Roman baths (never completed) and a huge hall or basilica that served as the audience chamber for a late-Roman imperial palace. And so the tale could go on, for the Romans were some of the greatest builders and engineers that the world has yet known, and their works have endured over the centuries.

Yet in all the empire it is Rome that has the greatest lure and makes the deepest impression on the mind. The buildings of Rome are built on a scale that dwarfs those of the other cities of the empire. Her temples and squares were the models upon which the buildings in the cities of North Africa and Gaul were built. To visit the echoing dome of the Pantheon or the shell of the huge Colosseum is to gain a deeper insight into the vast power and resources of the city that was the dominant political power in the world for four centuries, a city which, even after *Rome, mistress of the empire* it fell from power, was so mighty in its ruined desolation that it was to remain a symbol of man's past achievements in the ages that followed; to remain, too, an inspiration to the scholars and archaeologists who first began the serious study of man's past.

Table of Emperors

Main Emperors of the First and Second Centuries A.D.

Augustus	27 B.C.–A.D. 14
Tiberius	A.D. 14–37
Gaius	A.D. 37–41
Claudius	A.D. 41–54
Nero	A.D. 54–68
Period of Anarchy	A.D. 68–69
Vespasian	A.D. 69–79
Titus	A.D. 79–81
Domitian	A.D. 81–96
Nerva	A.D. 96–98
Trajan	A.D. 97–117
Hadrian	A.D. 117–138
Antoninus Pius	A.D. 138–161
Marcus Aurelius	A.D. 161–180
Commodus	A.D. 176–192
Period of Anarchy	A.D. 192–193
Severus	A.D. 193–211

Other Emperors Mentioned

Caracalla	A.D. 211–217
Diocletian	A.D. 284–305
Constantine	A.D. 306–337
Justinian	A.D. 527–565

Suggestions for Further Reading

General

F. R. Cowell, *Everyday Life in Ancient Rome* (Batsford, 2nd ed. 1962)

A. A. M. van der Heyden and H. H. Scullard, *Atlas of the Classical World* (Nelson, reprint 1967)

Sir Mortimer Wheeler, *Roman Art and Architecture* (Thames and Hudson, reprint 1968)

For those who wish to learn more about the subjects dealt with in the different chapters of this book:

Chapter 1

C. W. Ceram, *Gods, Graves and Scholars* (Gollancz, 1971)

Chapter 2

G. Webster, *Practical Excavation* (A. & C. Black, reprint 1965)

Chapter 3

A. R. Burn, *The Romans in Britain* (An anthology of inscriptions. (Blackwell, 2nd ed. 1969)

R. J. Charleston, *Roman Pottery* (Faber, 1965)

M. Grant, *Roman History from Coins* (Cambridge University Press, reprint 1968)

Chapter 4

G. Webster, *The Roman Imperial Army* (A. & C. Black, 1969)

Chapter 5

A. R. Birley, *Life in Roman Britain* (Batsford, 1964)

O. Brogan, *Roman Gaul* (G. Bell & Sons, 1953)

G. L. Harding, *The Antiquities of Jordan* (Lutterworth Press, 1959)

P. MacKendrick, *Romans on the Rhine* (Funk & Wagnalls, New York 1969—to be published by Dent)

A. Maiuri, *Pompeii* (Instituto Geografico de Agostini S.p.A., Novara, 1960)

S. Raven, *Rome in Africa* (Evans Brothers, 1969)

F. J. Wiseman, *Roman Spain* (G. Bell & Sons, 1956)

Index

110

112